THE ADVENTURE SERIES
SKIING

THE ADVENTURE SERIES

Anneka Rice
SCUBA-DIVING
SAILING

THE ADVENTURE SERIES
SKIING
ANNEKA RICE

Robson Books

Cartoons by Larry

Thanks to Esso for their support of the Adventure Series project.

First published in Great Britain in 1987 by Robson Books Ltd, Bolsover House, 5–6 Clipstone Street, London W1P 7EB.

British Library Cataloguing in Publication Data

Rice, Anneka
   Skiing. – (Adventure series).
   1. Skis and skiing
   I. Title II. Series
   796.93   GV854

ISBN 0-86051-461-7

Typeset by AKM Associates (UK) Ltd, Ajmal House, Hayes Road, Southall, London

Printed in Great Britain by St Edmundsbury Press Ltd, Bury St Edmunds, Suffolk

Bound by Dorstel Press Ltd, Harlow, Essex

Acknowledgements

Many people have helped me to learn to ski, and to put this book together. Ray Robinson was the photographer, and Mark Fishlock did a great deal of additional research. I would also like to thank Heinrich Wagner of the St Anton Tourist Office and Harold Roffner of the St Anton Ski School for all their help, and Professor Franz Hoppichler, the President of Interski, for his encouragement.

Thanks to these – and to everyone else.

Foreword

by Clive Freshwater
Chairman of the British Association
of Ski Instructors

This is just the level of book to encourage beginners to the sport of skiing.

An interesting and informative account of a first ski holiday with sound advice in its 'facts' section. It covers all aspects of safety and most sides of the technique for beginners. This is very cleverly brought out in Anneka's diary and explained in more detail in the rest of the text.

The progress of Anneka on her ski holiday highlights the reasons for taking qualified instruction from the start and enforces the advice given by Professor Franz Hoppichler on that point. I would highly recommend this to any person intent on their first ski holiday.

Introduction

I never thought that I would learn how to ski. For one thing, the skiing 'bug' seemed to have passed me by – films of ski jumpers, downhillers and even the antics of the freestyle skiers never spurred me on to find out how to do it myself. And, I must admit, my very first experience on the slopes had been a total disaster!

When I was eight years old, my father, who had done a fair amount of skiing during his army days, was determined to have a family holiday in the Austrian Alps. So after we saved up enough 6d's in a big glass jar, off we went to the picturesque village of Westendorf. Early the next morning, I was plonked down on a nursery slope, and my parents headed off for some 'real' skiing, full of anticipation and wearing the then-current ski boots resembling laced-up hockey boots.

After a short while, I became aware of a commotion, and then I saw a group of skiers making their way down the side of the mountain, carrying something on a kind of stretcher. That 'something' was my father, and although he insisted on making his way to the hotel under his own steam, he was later diagnosed as having broken *both* legs – and on his very first descent of the day!

That was the end of my skiing for the next 20 years. The Rice family never went on another winter skiing holiday, and I always politely declined friends' invitations to join them on the piste. My idea of a holiday was something much safer, like lying beside a swimming pool, getting brown.

Then my television work – especially *Wish You Were Here . . .?* – began to take me back to the mountains and the snow. However, a good camera operator and a carefully executed smile can make even the most rigid, unskilled and petrified beginner seem like a confident, carefree Franz Klammer. I found that, with practice and a gentle push, I could usually ski across the camera's field of vision, and even say a few words.

However, I began to feel that my faked schussing was not really fair to viewers, and besides, I was increasingly intrigued to discover exactly what the appeal was for the hundreds of thousands of skiers who travel to the Alps every year. So when a book and video about my attempts to learn to ski was proposed, I took a deep breath, pushed all my apprehension to the back of my mind – and agreed.

DAY 1

Why do flights to ski resorts always leave at such an ungodly hour? I got up at the crack of dawn, and attempted to greet the day with some vague excitement.

I'd tried to do as much preparation as possible beforehand. Full of trepidation I might be, but I didn't want to arrive unfit and without all the necessary gear as well. For the last time I did a few of the exercises (you will find these at the foot of this page and those that follow) that I'd been doing for the last month or so, and I could feel how much stronger my calf muscles and ankles were than they had been. It's surprising how, even in someone as active as I am, there are parts of the body that seem never to have been used before! I felt very fit, but would I be fit enough? (*Don't even* think *about broken legs.*)

We were heading for St Anton, near the famous Arlberg Pass in western Austria and the centre point of a region that encompasses the skiing villages of Lech, St Christoph, Stuben and Zürs. Although not at a very high altitude (for an Alpine resort) – it stands at 4,277 feet – it is overlooked by the majestic Valluga, which rises to a respectable 9,184 feet. People *actually* ski down that!

In photographs, St Anton looked the perfect quaint Tyrolean village, although with a permanent population of just over 2,100 (this soars during the season), it perhaps should be called a town. Full of charming, traditional architecture, the focal point is a church with a red 'onion' dome.

However, picture-postcard quaint-

Fitness training

You'll find that skiing makes demands on muscles and joints that you didn't even know you had! Because of this, it's worth carrying out a modest programme of fitness training before your holiday.

However, you don't have to endure agonizing daily workouts at your local gym. Instead, a few gentle exercises to increase your flexi-bility, strength and stamina, and performed whenever you have time, will prove extremely worthwhile – your body will certainly appreciate the thought when faced with its first 3-mile downhill run. In addition, well-tuned muscles and agile joints are less prone to injury, particularly the kinds of muscular strains that leave so many holidaymakers lying helplessly in hotel saunas or limping

ness (and the rumoured *après ski* haunts) aside, the primary reason why I chose to go to St Anton was that the Austrian teaching method is famous throughout the world for its extreme thoroughness. For example, the Austrians place great importance on learning to ski in clear, easy stages, making sure that beginners are comfortable and competent before progressing further. I liked the sound of that.

The ski school at St Anton, established by the influential Hannes Schneider in 1922, is said by some to be the strictest in the world, and going to learn to ski there is like going to Lords to learn

back dejectedly to the relative comforts of their hard Alpine beds. And you'll find that the air of the mountains is much thinner than it is further down, and will leave you feeling more tired than usual at the end of the day, so being in the best shape possible is important.

To skiers, the most important area of the body is below the waist. The knees and thighs are under almost constant stress, either making turns or determining posture. In particular, the knees are engaged in a constant battle with snow and ice, which are committed to up-ending the skier at every opportunity. To make this struggle even more one-sided, an icy slope can usually count on the assistance of its greatest ally, the force of gravity. Our own calves and ankles, too,

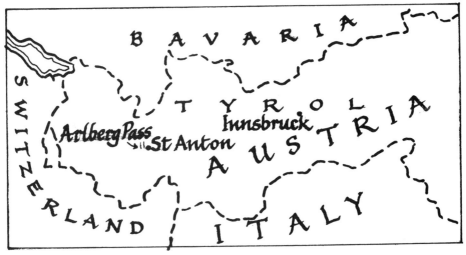

to play cricket or to New Orleans to learn trad jazz. In addition, a little way down the road is St Christoph, home of the Federal Ski School where instructors and others sponsored by the ski-conscious Austrian government are trained. Head of the school is Professor Franz Hoppichler, a mystical figure known as the 'Ski Pope' or *'Der Guru'*, and arrangements had been made for me to meet him tomorrow for some advice.

Five o'clock in the morning is not the ideal time to start packing, so I'd done most of it the night before. Why, then, did there seem to be so much left to go into my cases? I always like to travel light, but this is out of the question when going on a skiing holiday.

I'd visited a couple of shops specializing in skiwear, but had been overwhelmed by the amount of choice. It seemed *de rigueur* at the

come in for some heavy work.

Above the waist, although mobility is of greater importance than strength, stomach muscles (if firm enough) will help to drive the rest of the upper body more efficiently. Having strong arms may seem relatively unimportant to the novice skier, particularly after watching the experts race downhill and hardly use their light-weight poles. However, although you may have no intention of competing in the downhill at Wengen, you'll soon discover how vital the arms are when you try to make progress over flat ground. Here, gravity has mercifully ceased to send you careering downhill, but now all your locomotive power has to be produced by your arms. If they aren't strong enough, they'll soon be crying for help.

Day 1 continued

moment to dress in clothes so brightly coloured that you would glow in the dark. Now, I like to look cheerful, but not as cheerful as that . . .

Eventually I sorted out the three options for outer wear, all of which have to completely undress! It's bad enough battling in a cubicle in this country; in St Anton, I'd have to strip off not only the suit but also ski boots and thermal underwear, dropping my clothes into pools of melted snow. I also tried on

★★★
★ **Following the Stockholm Blood-bath in 1520, during which his father was massacred by the king, Gustav Vasa fled from Mora to Sälen. On the way, he was overtaken by a group of scouts and persuaded to return to Mora to lead a rebellion. This uprising** **was successful, and Vasa later took the throne as Gustavus I of Sweden. A massive race, covering a distance of more than 55 miles, now commemorates his return journey to Mora, and is entered by about 12,000 skiers every year.** ★
★★★

were made of synthetic fibre that, although waterproof, can 'breathe'. The one-piece ski suit resembles a padded boiler suit, is very warm and does not allow wet snow to drip in around the waist. As you can imagine, I'm quite an expert on boiler suits, and the major disadvantage is only too apparent when you're caught short. You an anorak and salopettes, the latter resembling padded dungarees, and finally, I looked at ski pants and anoraks; all these are worn with a pullover or a T-shirt.

As snow down the backside seemed a distinct possibility with the pants, I rejected them in favour of the one-piece – better the devil you know. Another important

You'll probably find that one side of your body is naturally stronger than the other. As all skiing manoeuvres involve strength and flexibility in both directions, it would be unhelpful to exaggerate this bias by overdeveloping your good side, so ensure that you exercise both equally. There is an argument for doing compensatory exercises on the weaker side, but if you're beginning to think in these terms, you're probably taking the whole business far too seriously!

Of course, many people will claim that they just don't have time. However, the following exercises are designed to fit as unobtrusively as possible into the pattern of a normal day. You could set aside some time to carry them out, but equally, many of them can be fitted into your

Day 1 continued

point is that you should stay away from 'wet look' clothes. Apparently, when these come in contact with snow and ice, there is virtually no friction, and you will slide and slide . . .

I knew that I would need a warm head covering – did you know that you lose about 20 per cent of your body heat through your scalp? – and I seemed to have a choice of two types: the traditional woolly 'bobble' hat, and the 'Lawrence of Arabia' wrap-round hood and headband. I chose the hood, though later I saw lots of people wearing just a headband.

Something for my hands came next. Mittens are warmer than gloves but make you a lot less dextrous, so unless the weather is really frosty or you suffer particularly badly from the cold, gloves are probably the best choice. You can always make them warmer by wearing a pair of thin thermal undergloves or silk liners; these are easy to stick in a pocket.

What you wear under your ski clothes is possibly more important than the ski clothes themselves. You will stay much warmer if you wear lots of thin layers than just a couple of thick ones. Thermal underwear – that is, a vest and long johns – is fairly essential if you are going to ski in mid-winter. However, wearing track suit bottoms under your ski pants or whatever can do just as well for your lower half. Don't forget to take plenty of socks. I decided on some thick, ribbed woolly walking socks and tennis socks – which turned out to be a mistake.

Also essential are sun glasses and goggles. The sunlight in the mountains is incredibly intense and is also reflected off the snow. Without sun glasses, your eyes can become extremely irritated, and you may be unfortunate enough to fall victim to snow blindness. If you can, buy a pair that also protects you around the sides and the top, and ones that

routine in such a way that it will not seem as if you're exercising at all.

Do all the exercises for as long as you feel you can, and then one or two more times (or a little bit longer). This way, you should be gradually increasing the number of times (or length of time) you can do each one – showing an increase in strength and fitness – while not rushing things, injuring yourself.

Stepping up
Some of the best exercises to do for the lower body involve simply stepping up on to a slightly raised platform. In the gym, this might be a low bench, but at home it can be a small stool or the first step of a staircase.

First, step up using your right foot and bring up your left foot to join it. Then step down with your

14

are tinted darker than you would normally wear during the summer.

Goggles that fit snugly to the face are needed for those days when the sun disappears and the snow falls. There is nothing more irritating than having to stop and wipe drips of melting snow off the inside of the lenses of your sun glasses – and it can be dangerous, since good vision on the slopes is essential to avoid hazards. Be sure to buy the anti-mist type.

Although I would be renting my equipment at St Anton, including ski boots, I knew that my normal footwear would be inadequate on the ice and snow on the roads and

left foot and follow it with your right. Repeat, alternating the leg you use to haul your weight up the step.

Now stand on the stair or a secure low platform with just the balls of the feet supporting the body. In this position, you can carry out a number of simple strengthening, stretching and balancing exercises.

With your weight evenly distrib- uted on both feet, rock up and down, contracting the tendons at the back of your legs as you go up and stretching them as you sink gently down. Then transfer your weight, first to your right foot and then to your left, as you go up and down. A minute or so of this each day will lead to a dramatic improve- ment in the strength and suppleness of your calves, and it will also help

develop your sense of balance.

Backs to the wall
This is the most famous ski exercise. In any drinking establishment where two or more skiers gather together, groups can regularly be found lined up against a wall, with their knees locked in combat.

Some will already have trembling thighs, and the faces of others will be contorted in agonized grimaces.

To reach this state, participants sit with their backs pressed up against the wall and their thighs at right angles to the vertical, as if sitting on a chair. There is, however, no chair, and much of the body's weight is supported by the muscles of the upper thighs.

This exercise is deceptive. At first, victims feel very comfortable,

Day 1 continued

paths there. At a friend's suggestion, I'd invested in a pair of enormous, soft, padded 'moon boots' with grip soles. For a joke, I'd tried on a pair of the hairy ones, which thankfully are now out of fashion – I looked as if I had trodden on two Old English sheepdogs!

I also needed sun cream and lip salve. Unless you are very fair-skinned, you should take along a

and are happy to stay in this position for the rest of the evening. However, it's not long before the thighs begin to shudder, and you can almost see the strength draining from the aching tissue as the off-duty skiers press their backs harder against the wall in an attempt to enlist greater assistance from friction. One by one, the contestants find that they can't take the agony any longer and crumple in a heap of quivering limbs and sweated brows.

Holiday skiers are not advised to take up this exercise competitively, but you may find it useful if you attempt it for only as long as you feel comfortable. Initially, this may be for periods as short as 30 seconds, but with regular practice, you can usually build up endurance times of $1\frac{1}{2}$ minutes or more.

Day 1 continued

cream with the same sunscreen factor that you would use on a beach; however, if you burn easily, take one that is stronger. If unprotected, your lips will become dry and chapped from the wind, cold and sunlight, and from the dehydration that occurs at high altitudes. Lip salve should be used as a precaution, from the very first day, for once your lips are sore, it is really too late. Moisturizing cream is also a good idea, to repair the damage done during the day and to provide protection when you next hit the slopes.

A friend gave me a good-luck present just before I left, one that I later found invaluable. This was a 'bumbag', which resembled a soft waterproof banana. It is tied on round the waist, with the bag resting on your bottom (hence the name), and can hold all sorts of useful small things such as lip salve, camera and film, sun cream, undergloves. However, it can be

less than useful if you spend most of your day's skiing sitting down, which is something all beginners do, so an alternative is a small, light-weight, waterproof rucksack.

It is both unpleasant and unwise to ski in damp clothing, and it would be a shame to lose a precious day of your holiday while you wait for your things to dry out, so take spares of anything that can get wet. It is also a good idea to take along a few warmer things; even if you ski at the end of the season, the weather can change dramatically and unexpectedly.

Arm strengthening

Most slopes go up as well as down, and there will be many occasions when you need to propel yourself against the force of gravity. In addition, you'll have to lift and carry your skis a lot. This is when strong arms are an asset.

To this end, conventional press-ups are as good an exercise as any. Women may prefer an alternative to the traditional horizontal method, instead pressing up at an angle against a table, the back of a chair or a sturdy work surface. The result is more comfortable and equally effective.

Flexibility

During the course of your training, you'll be asked to twist your body into a number of positions, a few of

Day 1 continued

which you'll swear are physical impossibilities. In some, your body will be desperate to unwind like a twisted rubber band, but somehow you'll have to learn to be comfortable while so strangely contorted. For this, flexibility exercises are important – first, to lessen the pain of achieving the correct position, and then to be able to maintain it.

Sit-ups are simple exercises that can be performed at home. Lie on your back on the floor, keeping your legs bent. Hook your feet under a chair or similar to keep them flat on the floor, or else ask a friend to hold them down.

Remember, once you have hauled yourself into the upright position, returning safely to the horizontal is equally important. This shouldn't consist of a loud exhalation followed

Day 1 continued

Insurance

Arranging insurance can be a mine-field when it comes to skiing. Compared to a conventional holiday, injury is far more likely – both to yourself and others – and it is imperative to be adequately covered. This can be a quite complex business.

If you book your holiday through a tour operator, an insurance policy will usually be offered or will be part of the package. However, you can often opt out and make your own arrangements. The insurance cover you'll need falls into five main categories:

• *Cancellation* If your holiday is cancelled for some reason – e.g. sickness, accident, jury service – you're liable to lose any deposit you might have paid.

• *Personal accident* This is usually a lump-sum settlement.

• *Medical expenses* These can arise out of an accident (broken bones, etc.) or sickness, or you may need emergency dental treatment.

• *Personal liability* This gives you cover against claims made against you by a third party. You should be careful to have adequate insurance for this as holiday-makers have been sued for huge damages after causing serious

Somehow I got all of this into my case, as well as a few pieces of finery for the promised *après ski*. I ran through my checklist to make sure that I hadn't forgotten anything. I had: my passport photo (for the ski pass) and the details of my insurance (there's a checklist opposite). As I rushed to retrieve them, the doorbell rang – the taxi to take me to the airport. I was now a nervous wreck!

Gatwick on winter weekends is awash with the sight and sounds of returning skiers, all gleaming teeth and healthy tans, and the

by a crash to the floor! Instead, try to imagine the vertebrae of your spine slowly unwinding, while you use your stomach muscles to make a controlled return to the floor. For extra flexibility, twisting to either side as you go up will expand the basic routine.

An exercise that's virtually the reverse of the sit-up is the back curl. Lie on your stomach on the floor with your arms at your sides, pointing towards your feet. Lift your head and legs off the floor. Your spine will form a concave arch, a result of the contraction of the muscles of the back and the stretching of those in front.

Squat-jump-thrust
From a standing position, lower yourself into a deep squat so that

Insurance

injury to, or the death of, a fellow skier.

• *Loss of personal baggage and/or money* It is advisable to check the wording of a policy thoroughly before you purchase it, looking for exemption clauses, excesses that may need to be paid and limits of cover. You may find that your personal household insurance covers certain items for travel in Europe. In addition, when hiring skis or other equipment, ask whether the shop has insured it for your use, or whether you have to pay for any damage or loss out of your own pocket.

Once you have purchased your insurance, it's important to make sure that you have a contact number for your insurer, and that they're available 24 hours a day, seven days a week, so that any claim or query can be answered immediately (in most countries, medical treatment will be refused unless you can give prior evidence of a means of payment). You should also make sure that, if you're travelling in a party, someone else has the contact number as well as details of your policy.

The golden rule is: make sure you know exactly what you're covered for and the correct procedures for making a claim.

---

clatter of equipment and the telling of tales of Alpine disasters and triumphs. Mooching around quietly on the sidelines are the beginners who, like me, are only now starting to realize just what they have let themselves in for.

I met up with the director and the camera crew, who all seemed in good humour and looking forward to the expedition far more than I – but then *they* didn't have to learn to ski. Comments flowed like 'Oh, well, if you break a leg, at least it'll be on film. We can send it to ITN – make a nice piece!' The trouble was, they weren't joking!

your knees touch your chest. You may need to thrust both arms forward to maintain your balance. Then, slowly and smoothly, rise up until you're standing again. The key to this exercise is keeping the soles of the feet firmly in contact with the floor.

The next exercise involves imitating a rabbit, and is known as the 'squat jump'. Squat down and then jump up as high as you can in both a forward and sideways direction. This is particularly good for the thighs and knees, but not so good for public relations if attempted in a crowd.

The squat is also the starting point for one of the most universally feared exercises – the 'squat thrust', which has reduced trained athletes to gibbering wrecks. From a low

Day 1 continued

Our flight to Zurich, the nearest airport to St Anton, was called and we were truly on our way.

From an aesthetic point of view, there can be no better way to start a skiing holiday than by flying over the Alps on a clear sunny day. The valleys, dotted with little towns and villages, are beautiful, but the mountains are what really grab your attention. However, as I gazed at these soaring peaks, I gulped as it struck me that they were probably similar to ones I would find at my destination, and which I would be expected to ski down . . .

We arrived safely, without incident and, from the airport, we caught a train to St Anton – a journey that took us through

miles and miles of picture-postcard Alpine countryside, over fast-flowing rivers traversed by traditional wooden bridges, through mountain villages and dark, thick pine forests. By the time we arrived, dusk had fallen and it had become quite cold.

As I hauled down my luggage, I wished that I'd been able to travel lighter, even though I knew that I'd brought very little with me that wasn't necessary. However,

squat, place both hands on the floor in front of you, and then extend your legs behind you. Push up with your feet and bend your knees to bring the latter forward to touch your elbows, then stretch out your legs again.

The squat thrust will make your legs hurt and your heart beat faster, so on that evidence alone, it must be doing you some good!

Sitting and standing
There are two good exercises that can be done whenever you're sitting or standing – and with the minimum of embarrassment.

If you're sitting down, place both feet flat on the floor and press down with the soles. For an exercise which, on the face of it, involves such an extraordinary lack of activity, you'll soon feel which muscles

Day 1 continued

as I watched my fellow passengers, I saw that I was much better off than those who had also brought their own equipment – boots, skis and poles that fell over, swung out dangerously and needed a third hand to handle. Still, the absolutely *wonderful* mountain air did a lot to revive us all, and the locals must have thought we looked a load of idiots as we all stood motionless and took exaggerated deep breaths.

By the time I had checked into the hotel and reached my room, I was in a muddle. Should I go and gulp in more gallons of mountain air, have a sauna or have a drink? The crew headed for the bar; I headed for the sauna. 'CLOSED.' Oh, well – tomorrow!

are receiving proper attention.

If you're standing, tilt forward as far as you can while keeping your feet flat on the floor, then lean back; now repeat. It may seem like a small effort, but this exercise acts most effectively on the calves, knees and thighs.

Inconspicuous exercise
Even the busiest person can, with a little imagination, fit a few modest exertions into the pattern of the working day.

For example, while riding up an escalator in an underground station or a department store, you can, relatively inconspicuously, carry out the stepping up and tilting-forward exercises described above, using your bag or briefcase as a counter-balance. It's true that, on the way

Day 1 continued

★★★

All in the stars?

Those born under the star sign of Pisces (19 February–20 March) are reputed to be calm, thoughtful, creative, flexible and attracted to the romantic. Perhaps this combination is responsible for the curious fact that many of the world's top skiers of recent years are Pisceans.

For example, World Cup champions Ingemar Stenmark of Sweden and Andreas Wenzel of Liechtenstein were both born on 18 March; the legendary Swede in 1956; Wenzel, two years later. Top women skiers, Marie-Thérèse Nadig and Erika Hess, both from Switzerland, would also be part of the Pisces racing team. Marie-Thérèse came into the world on 8 March 1954, while Erika is almost exactly eight years her junior, having been born on 6 March 1962.

Other members of this impressive line-up would include the brilliant Austrian Leonhard Stock (14 March 1956), and Maria Epple, one of West Germany's skiing Epple sisters (11 March 1959), while Paeola de Chiesa of Italy (14 March 1956), Austrian downhiller Erwin Resch (4 March 1961) and Max Julen (15 March 1961), Swiss star of the giant slalom, would also compete in the Pisces team colours.

down, you'll have to step and rock while facing the person behind you, but - who knows? - he or she could be a skiing enthusiast, too.

Once you get into the habit of inconspicuous exercise, your imagination tends to run wild. Other opportunities for undercover training include walking instead of using some sort of transport, bending your knees to take things from low shelves or bottom drawers (this is also much better for your back) and stretching with alternate arms to reach objects high up. In this way, you'd probably be doing the equivalent of a thirty-minute programme of stamina and flexibility exercises without ever having to set aside the time.

The minutes spent standing in a lift watching the floor numbers flashing is time that could be more productively spent climbing the stairs. This doesn't mean running like a maniac, but calmly walking, toning the legs as you go and working out the heart and lungs

into the bargain.

One of the best forms of exercise, and one that's particularly relevant to skiers, is simply walking over uneven terrain. A good stroll on a heath or beach or over waste ground or cobblestones will quickly improve your balance, agility and general stamina.

If you can stand the embarrassment of being spotted, take your ski poles and practise the skier's walking rhythm: right foot, left pole and so on.

Many accidents occur as a result of fatigue, mainly because it seriously impairs the powers of concentration. It's unwise and unenjoyable to ski when you're exhausted, so some time spent building up strength and stamina at home can reap untold benefits in the mountains. The pleasure of being able to ski all day long without too many painful after-effects is the goal of every holiday skier. Once on the snow, your body will appreciate the trouble you have taken beforehand.

DAY 2

Proper continental quilts are better than Mogadon. I woke up having had ten hours of the deepest sleep that I can remember. If I could find a way of bottling bedding, I'd be a millionaire overnight.

I needed to get to the equipment shop and be kitted out before ski school started at 9.30. The hotel corridors were already humming with activity, as brightly clad guests bustled by, all eager to be the first in the queue at the cable-car station. I dressed hurriedly and went down to the breakfast room, which looked like the headquarters of a training programme for the next Super Race, everyone looking incredibly healthy with tanned faces and clear eyes. There was quite a din as the day's campaigns were methodically planned.

Breakfast is the skier's most important meal of the day and, in Austria, they certainly know how to serve it in style. No cold, burned toast which crumbles as you try to butter it. No eggs and bacon, baked beans and fried bread, all swimming in a sea of grease. Instead, a table in the corner was decked out with all kinds of cereal, sides of ham and other cold meats, a huge, round cheese, fruit, yoghurt, black bread and jam. This spread was like a harvest festival offering, and although I rarely eat breakfast at home, I couldn't resist attacking what was on offer with relish.

Soon after I sat down, the other guests began to leave, and I could see that they were concerned about the skiing time being wasted with every extra cup of coffee. It seemed a rather uncivilized way to

Your equipment

If you are going on your first skiing holiday, it's a good idea to hire your equipment. You may find that, after all, you are not cut out to be Franz Klammer and you don't want to be left with a cupboard full of expensive skis, poles and boots, all destined for the small ads in your local paper. On the other hand, if you are sure that skiing is for you and you want to buy your own equipment, it is best to do so before you leave home if you want to avoid paying the high prices charged at resorts.

On this holiday, I hired my equipment from Tony Pangratz, telling him that I was complete beginner and needed all the basics. He disappeared into the back of the shop and returned with a smart pair of

Day 2 continued

very sophisticated-looking boots, consisting of an outer part made of hard plastic and an inner soft boot. He undid clips on each of the boots and they slid open at the rear.

As I prepared to try them on, Tony stopped me. 'You're wearing the wrong type of socks,' he said. 'Yours are ribbed, too many wrinkles.'

Socks are not something I had ever given much thought to before, but as I was to discover, a good ski sock needs to be elastic and smooth on the inside. 'So many people complain that their boots are uncomfortable, when it is actually their socks that are wrong.' Tony explained. I bought a few pairs of the proper kind.

I was then clamped into the boots, which felt both comfortable and secure. Boot technology has come a

Day 2 continued

start the day. Why the rush? I thought this was supposed to be a holiday . . . However, although I didn't know it then, within days I too would be raring to go after packing in as much energy from the hotel's spread as I could in as short a time as possible.

As I left the hotel, I was hit by a tidal wave of glorious mountain air. The orchestra swells, the camera pulls back – *look out, here comes Julie Andrews!*

long way since my father faced the slopes in lace-up boots.

I walked around the shop for a while to test my new footwear. When hiring or buying a pair of boots, it is important to make sure that you give them a good tryout in the shop – some experts say you should walk around in them for half an hour – before deciding. Boots are perhaps your most important piece of equipment: they have to protect your feet and ankles as well as transfer the movement of your legs to your skis. You will soon regret it if you settle for a pair that don't fit properly or simply feel uncomfortable.

Tony asked me to lean forward towards the front of the boot lugs, and was satisfied when I told him that there was no pain on my shins.

Day 2 continued

I joined the exodus of spirited skiers, not really knowing where I was going. At first view, at least, St Anton was certainly living up to its brochure image.

All the pavements, if there were any, were buried beneath deep snow, and the colourful crowd strode boldly down the middle of the street past ski equipment, food and souvenir shops, chemists and bars, drawing occasional hoots from the less purposeful flow of cars.

Ski boots make a strange 'squeezing' sound on snow, like the squeak

'Boots for beginners are softer and more flexible than those for good skiers,' he said. Mine felt restrictive enough already, but I was comforted by the fact that, as there was so little movement inside the boots; my fragile ankles would be well supported.

The next item on the agenda was skis. Walking uneasily in my new boots, I followed Tony into the back room where he showed me an impressive selection of all makes, lengths and colours. There was even a pair that could have been no longer than three feet and must have been meant for a child - or a very bad beginner. Tony chose a pair which were just a few inches over my height and also quite flexible. Skis of this length and rigidity are recommended for beginners because they are easier to turn.

of new leather. St Anton's other distinctive sound – that of cars fitted with snow chains – probably goes some way towards reducing the number of road accidents there. You can hear the approaching clatter of the chains from quite a long way off.

My first stop was Tony Pangratz's equipment hire shop on the high street, where I was kitted out (*described below*). Before I left, Tony gave me a pass which enabled me to leave my equipment at his small shop and store next to the ski school – something I

Tony told me that his father used to make skis by hand, a dwindling craft in Alpine regions today. 'These days,' he said dismissively, 'they are made by computer.' In fact, ski equipment has become so sophisticated that skis and bindings designed only 15 years ago now look quite primitive by comparison.

Tony's assistant, Patrick, checked the sharpness of the skis' metal edges before clamping them to a bench and setting the bindings. Modern bindings have made skiing a much less hazardous sport in recent years, and are set individually, according to the weight and ability of the skier. After I had taken them off, Patrick fixed one of my boots into a binding, made his adjustments and swivelled the boot sideways. I was very pleased to see

was to appreciate more and more as the week flew by.

The only way not to walk like one of the Woodentops is to undo the clips on your boots, which at least allows you to bend your ankles. Assuming that you're unlucky enough to have to carry your own skis (and unless you're Joan Collins, you'll have to), the correct way is over your shoulder with the tips (front ends) down. This is hard work and will justify the arm exercises that you did before you left home (you *did* do them, didn't you?). With my skis out of harm's way, I rejoined the flow of human traffic and set off in what I assumed was the direction of the ski school.

A chaotic collection of primary colours and loud laughter indicated that I had arrived. Skiers were being organized into groups, those who professed some basic ability being tested to confirm their claims . . . or expose their bravado. This was my first encounter with the Austrians' famous thoroughness, making sure that no one was put into a class that would be too difficult for them.

I looked around for the 'Ski Pope', who was to meet me here. As head of the Federal Ski School at St Christoph, which trains

the binding release it cleanly and easily. Patrick then repeated the operation with my other boot.

The binding mechanism is designed to come away from the clips at either the front or the rear if it is subjected to a certain amount of sideways force. On the other hand, the boot is held quite securely against forward and backward pressure, so that you can lean quite a long way over the front of your skis without falling over. In this position, you look like a circus clown in giant shoes.

Another development in the design of bindings is the 'ski stopper' or 'ski brake'. This looks like a spur and is built into the binding. Stoppers not only prevent the ski from disappearing down the mountain if you lose it in a fall, they also provide

instructors to a level which puts them among the most accomplished and knowledgeable of skiers, Professor Franz Hoppichler's reputation has spread all over the world. He had also recently become president of Interski, the international body that aims to improve both ski technique and instruction. If you want advice about skiing, you can't go much higher than the 'Pope'.

I spotted the Professor, a craggily handsome and very fit-looking

an effective means of fastening both skis together when you have to carry them. Older designs had restraining straps - cords that you tied to your boot. Isn't progress a wonderful thing?

The last pieces of equipment I needed were ski poles. To find the right length, I was told to turn the pole upside down and grip it just underneath the 'basket', the circular plastic 'snowflake' on the bottom of the pole that prevents it from sinking too far into the snow. If your forearm remains parallel with the floor when you grip it in this way, the pole is the correct length.

The most common type of grip is a single handle with a looped safety strap. An alternative incorporates a moulded grip, like the guard you would find on the handle of a cutlass. The curved plastic 'claw' encloses part of the hand.

Skis

'Ski' is a Norwegian word, derived from the Norse word *skidh*, which means 'a piece of wood'. The correct Norwegian pronunciation is '*shee*'.

Over the centuries, skis have taken many shapes. Perhaps the most unusual were the 'goon skis', invented by Olympic figure skater Jimmy Madden in 1940. These 1.5-metre skis turned up at both ends,

and the wearer didn't know whether he was coming or going. Sadly, they didn't catch on.

After World War II, two manufact-urers on different sides of the Atlantic turned from building air-craft to work simultaneously on a design for a modern compound ski. In Britain, the Gomme firm, more used to constructing fusilage and wing parts, produced a ski consist-ing of a compressed soft wood top,

man in his late 50s or early 60s, and introduced myself. He suggested that I join a class for two or three days, and then take some private lessons towards the end of the week. 'Classes are great fun and will give you confidence,' he said, 'but individual instruction would help you make much faster progress. And what you needed is a *good* instructor, not a *nice* one . . .'

The 'Ski Pope' pointed me in the direction of the registration desk, and we made our farewells. After registering, and officially admitting that I was a complete novice on the slopes, I joined my class. It was only by chance that we were all from the UK. It is quite common for people from different countries to be put in classes together as the instructors almost invariably speak at least two other languages – usually English and French – besides their own native German.

The eight other beginners and I apprehensively eyed our instructor, one of the many at the St Anton Ski School. I was later to learn that Peter, a breezy young Tyrolean, had been born in St Anton and, apart from a few years spent away at university, had lived there all his life. He was a true child of the mountains – skiing in the winter and mountaineering in the summer – and the vast Arlberg region was as familiar to him as his own back garden.

In nervous anticipation, we lined up in front of Peter. We were a very mixed bunch. Brian and Liz were in their 40s, and while he seemed to be looking forward to the experience, it was obvious that Liz did not share her husband's irrepressible enthusiasm. Neil, a young lawyer, looked as if he was going to take the whole business terribly seriously. Ian and Belinda had arrived fresh from a few

a core impregnated with a polymer, and an aluminium sole. In the United States, the Head company used aircraft aluminium to make a ski with a thin aluminium top, a wood block core and an aluminium alloy sole.

Both skis had promising starts in life: the Head ski was particularly good on pistes, the Gomme excelled in powder. However, there were problems. The Head variety tended to delaminate when it hit bumps in very low temperatures, while the Gomme design soon became deformed, losing its arch and becoming unmanageable. As a result, the Gomme became part of the British industrial history, while the Head surged forward, having set a pattern that the ski manufacturing industry was later to follow and build upon.

Skis travel faster when in contact with the snow, providing they are

sessions on a dry slope in Halifax – preparation they both were to recommend heartily as it not only allowed them to get used to the feel of the strange equipment, but also helped them to grasp the theory behind the first few basic manoeuvres. Joanne was a quiet girl from Northern Ireland, and Carey's obvious pleasure in her surroundings fitted well with my image of what skiing should be like.

correctly waxed and the skier is in the tucked racing position. The longer the skis spend in the air during a race, the slower the time will be. Weight and flexibility are also important. Downhill skis are heavier and more rigid than those used for slalom events; slalom racers need the extra softness for easier turning.

As well as skis for snow and water, a relative newcomer is the grass ski, first produced in 1963 by Kurt Kaiser, a German knitting machine manufacturer. Also called 'roller skis', they are slightly longer than ice skates and have caterpillar tracks on the bottoms. Grass skiing was introduced to the UK in 1970; the first world championships – comprising a grass slalom and giant slalom – being held in 1979.

Day 2 continued

The final member of the class was Andy, a chartered accountant from London, who had turned up wearing a Barbour and cords. Peter advised him to get some waterproof clothing. As Andy had already fallen over four times before even getting his skis on, this made good sense.

Peter passed down the line, checking our skis and bindings – or *bindungs* as he called them. Ian's skis had not been waxed properly, and Peter told him to take them back to the ski hire shop to be redone. This came as a bit of surprise to me, as I'd always thought that the question of waxing was one that only bothered experts and poseurs. Apparently, even the skis of absolute beginners need to be correctly waxed, and everyone should always check with the hire shop to make sure that this has been done.

We were then instructed to 'Put your boots into your *bindungs*,' and for me, this proved to be one of the most difficult exercises of the morning. However, I did forget to make sure that the mechanism was completely open before trying to clamp in my boot. Watch out for that. You can bash the snow off your boot as much as you like and look very professional, but if the binding isn't open, your boot will never go in. In the end, I was the last one to get my skis on, and only after calling for help!

Peter then showed us how to hold the poles by putting the hand

Ski poles

At the beginning of the century, there were heated arguments over the relative merits of using one pole or two. In the first Kandahar downhill race in 1911, the winner Cecil Hopkinson struck a blow for the two-pole lobby, which has not looked back since.

Today, ski poles are often shaped to fit round the curves of the racer's body. This makes the skier more aerodynamic and so increases speed. Downhill racers use poles with smaller baskets than slalom skiers because the downhill skier is less likely to thrust his poles into deep snow.

The fall line, an imaginary line that a snowball would follow if you rolled it from the top, is the most direct route down the mountain.

through the strap and gripping the handle, so that the strap passes between the thumb and forefinger and is held across the palm of the hand. While I was learning all these initial basics, I began to appreciate being in a class where you can watch other people and learn from their mistakes. No doubt everybody would learn a lot from mine . . .

At last we were all kitted up and ready to do battle with the slope. Before that, however, Peter took us through some exercises so that we could familiarize ourselves with the surface and with our skis. First, we were told to stamp up and down 'like an elephant'. The extra weight on the bottoms of my feet soon made me feel as if I were walking through glue. Next, we rested on our poles and slid alternate feet forwards and backwards. Then, to limber us up, we

Saunas

Saunas are a part of everyday life on the Continent. Unlike mixed saunas in health clubs and spas in Great Britain where purple and sweating patrons sit clad in sensible bathing suits, studiously avoiding each others' gaze, modesty is thrown to the winds on the other side of the Channel. There it is considered unhygenic to even wrap a towel around yourself, and the sauna becomes a meeting point for more naked flesh than one usually sees in a lifetime. I saw my film crew in a completely different light!

Originating in Scandinavia, *ski jöring* is a cross between water skiing and a chariot race. All you have to do is strap on your skis, harness yourself to a galloping horse and shout: 'Hi, ho, Silver!' Not recommended for the fainthearted.

Day 2 continued

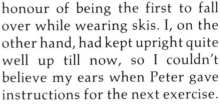

had to put our hands on our hips and swivel in a circular motion, as if using a hula hoop. This was all very frustrating. *Let's get going!*

However, Peter wasn't finished with his preliminaries yet. Next he told us to support ourselves on our poles and jump, taking both feet off the ground. Peter demonstrated: his jump was high and smooth. Mine felt as if my skis had been fixed to the ground by a piece of taut elastic – an ugly little jump of about eight inches or so – and I clattered back to the ground with a couple of loud *cracks*.

Off we went for a walk. Liz, who had been looking uneasy all morning, decided to claim the

honour of being the first to fall over while wearing skis. I, on the other hand, had kept upright quite well up till now, so I couldn't believe my ears when Peter gave instructions for the next exercise.

'Fall over,' he said.

How can he do this to us? I asked myself. And it was to prove a lot easier said than done. I gritted my teeth and toppled to one side, trying to overcome my natural inclination to catch myself as I fell.

However, no sooner had I settled on the snow than Peter was showing us how to get up. He first told us to put our skis, held parallel to each other, across the 'fall line' (*see page 36*), which with Peter's Tyrolean accent sounded disconcertingly like 'Put your skis across the *fraulein*'! When we were in position, we had to plant both poles into the snow by the hip on the uphill side. Then we placed the hand nearest the ground on to the poles just above the baskets, and the other

History highlights

• The earliest-known skis – dating from about 2,500 BC – were found in a peat bog in Hoting in Sweden. Probably used by hunters, they were more than 3 feet long and about 8 inches wide.
• A cave painting depicting two hunters on skis and estimated to be almost 4,000 years old was found at Roedoey in the north of Norway. Similar primitive paintings have been found in caves in northern Russia.

• An entry in the official history of the T'ang dynasty of China (AD 618-907) – a work called the *T'ang hui yao* –tells of a Mongol tribe that is said to 'skim over ice on wooden horses'. These primitive skis are described as being 6 inches wide and 'seven working boots long'.

Getting up from a fall

• Place skis parallel across fall line.

• Plant both poles by hip on uphill side.

• Place one hand on poles just above baskets and other on top of shafts.

• Push down on poles and lift yourself upright.

• In the 8th century, a Lombard, writing in Latin, told of hunters 'leaping forward on contrivances of wood curved like a bow'.

• The Vikings, who flourished from the late 8th century to the 10th, had a god and goddess of skiing.

• The first recorded military use of skis was at the Battle of Isen near Oslo in 1200.

• Among the illustrations on a map drawn in 1280 are ones showing a man on skis in Norway and a 'horse-footed man' in China.

• In Britain before the Industrial Revolution, when a new network of roads was built, many of them reaching out into previously inaccessible areas, people used to travel on 'skees' during adverse weather conditions.

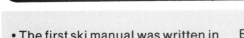

• The first ski manual was written in 1733 by Captain Jens Emmahusen of Trondheim for use by the Norwegian army. Troops then wore one long ski and one short ski, or *andor*, which was covered in fur.

• Skiing was introduced to the United States by an extraordinary character, 'Snowshoe' Thompson.

Born Jon Thorsteinson in 1827 in the Norwegian town of Telemark, he and his parents emigrated to America when he was ten years old, but it wasn't until the middle of the century, following the California Gold Rush that he found his true niche in American society. For 20 years, until his death in 1876, he doggedly carried the miners' mail to and from Carson City in Nevada

Day 2 continued

hand on top of the shafts. In theory, by pushing down on the poles, we were able to lift ourselves upright, but I couldn't seem to apply enough strength in the right direction, and even with the help of a few extra hands (and a few good-natured laughs), I was the last one in the class to get up. (Even by the end of the week, I still had not mastered this.)

We then took it in turns to walk towards Peter while, at the same time, raising our hands in the air and bringing them down to touch our knees. *This is taking hero worship a bit far!* I thought. My body was not very relaxed, and so my bends, instead of being smooth and flowing, were rather robot-like.

Before you can go down, you have to learn how to go up. To accomplish this, Peter showed us the technique of *sidestepping*. The name explains it all: with the skis placed across the fall line and using the poles for support, you simply

---

Sidestepping

• *Place skis parallel across fall line.*
• *Using poles for support, walk up sideways, taking small steps.*
• *As slope steepens, push knees further into mountain to edge skis.*

---

walk sideways up the mountain in a series of small steps. If you try to use larger ones to speed up the process, not only is there a danger of walking into your poles, it is also a lot more tiring. And as the slope gets steeper, you have to push your knees harder towards the mountainside so that your ski edges get an extra bite and thus grip better. When sidestepping, progress seems agonizingly slow, but it is safe and effective.

Each of us then skied downhill in a straight run, moving one ski to the side to turn and stop – our first attempts at *real* skiing. However, our elation was shortlived

---

and Placerville in California, his route taking him around the southern rim of Lake Tahoe and over the snowy Sierra Nevada mountains. To help him in his task, he wore home-made skis, made of oak and over 9 feet long.

• The first aerial somersault was recorded in Norway in 1909.

• The first history of skiing was written by Arnold Lunn in 1927, and inventively entitled *The History of Skiing*.

• Britain's first dry ski school was opened at Lillywhite's in London in 1932.

• The first double flip on skis was performed by the Austrian gymnast Hermann Goellner in 1965.

41

Ski families

Whether there is actually a 'ski gene' that can be passed on or whether the skiing activities of parents greatly influence their children, it certainly is true that it is relatively common for members of the same family to be interested -and occasionally to excel - in skiing.

The tiny state of Liechtenstein, huddling between the borders of Austria and Switzerland, is now the home of one of the most famous and successful skiing families in the world: the German-born Wenzels. In 1980, Andreas won the men's overall World Cup title, while in the same year, his sister Hanny claimed the honour in the women's competition. In addition, their younger

Day 2 continued

as, after each run (which lasted only seconds), we had to spend minutes sidestepping back up the hill and even longer waiting for the next turn. This was by far the most exhausting part of the morning; after what seemed like hours of continuous sidestepping, my legs and ankles were ready to give up and head for the sauna that was beckoning me back at the hotel. The waiting became excruciatingly boring, but to be fair to Peter, he was only trying to teach and advise everyone very thoroughly.

My problems all seemed to be above the waist. 'Anneka,' Peter said, 'your arms are all over the place, and your poles are waving around like a helicopter. If you'd been on a crowded piste, you'd have skewered at least half a dozen eyes by now!'

I soon came to realize that the position of the ski poles can quickly betray a nervous beginner. They should be held in a relaxed way, in front, with the tips pointing towards the heels of the skis. The minute the arms become tense, the grip on the poles tightens and forces the points up and out.

Despite Peter's remarks, I was quietly pleased with my progress. Yet it seems to be human nature to find solace in the fact that someone else is performing worse than you are, and here on the St Anton mountainside, Liz was now taking that role. I did sympathize with her difficulty in keeping her feet. At the first sign of trouble, there is a great temptation to sit

sisters Petra and Monika are accomplished competition skiers, although not with quite the same success.

The Epple sisters of West Germany are also justifiably acclaimed. Irene is famous for her efforts as a downhill racer and in the giant slalom, winning the latter at Saalbach and Val d'Isère in 1980 and a silver medal at the Olympics in the same year. Her sister Maria, two years her junior, had her first World Cup win in the giant slalom at Zweisel in 1981, and came second to Irene in this World Cup event the following year.

Twins often mirror each other in surprising ways, and this is true of the American skiing twins, Phil and Steve Mahre. Their skill was once measured in a specially organized

Snow plough

- Press ankles and knees inward to put skis on inside edges.
- Push out heels and keep tips together, making a V shape. Keep knees pressed inward.

- To pick up speed, flatten skis to snow by pushing out knees as if riding a horse.
- Speed will also increase if you make a narrower plough.

'head-to-head' slalom at Cortina in Italy. Although Phil is four minutes older than his brother, he had to concede the race to the younger man by 0.08 seconds.

Amiable Swiss slalom star Joel Gaspoz clearly loves a life of speed, for when not hurtling through slalom gates, he can often be found astride his second love – his motorcycle. Joel's desire for a life in the fast lane may have something to do with his father, who is a former Swiss regional slalom champion. Gaspoz *père* has slowed up somewhat in recent years, having swapped gates for plates at the restaurant he now owns. Brilliant Yugoslav racer Bojan Krizaj also comes from good skiing stock – *his* father was a national champion.

down: you want to get as close as you can to the security of the ground, before picking up any more speed. That morning, Liz seemed to spend more time on her back than on her skis.

Now came the infamous *snow plough*. Even people who have never skied before usually know this one; ski tips pointing at each other and the heels pushed apart. While some authorities – mainly the French – argue that the snow plough is an unnecessary exercise and actually a hindrance to learn-ing, it *is* a good safety measure because it allows you to control your speed very effectively. It's a very natural movement: as you push your legs wide apart from the heels, keeping your ski tips together at the front, your feet will naturally tilt inwards, dig-ging the skis' inside edges into the snow and breaking your speed by pushing the snow away from you. If you stop pushing and

straighten your whole body up, your skis will naturally slip back to a parallel position and you'll pick up speed very quickly. Just by pushing your ankles away from you again, you'll slow down. Very effective, but *not* very elegant! It was a ridiculous sight, the nine of us pushing our knees inwards so that we all looked knock-kneed.

I couldn't believe the intensity of the sun, and was glad that I'd brought my sun glasses – the reflection off the white snow was dazzling.

Despite the gargantuan break-fast I'd had, lunch had never been more welcome. We went to the restaurant at the railway station, which we had been told served the best cheap food in St Anton. It was also nearby, so we didn't have to walk too far.

The restaurant was alive with conversation. As I passed between the tables, I heard snippets like: 'I

And while there may be skiing dynasties, the athletic urge may appear in different guises from generation to generation. Take, for example, the parents of World Cup downhill champion Peter Mueller – they were Swiss champions at . . . badminton.

was leaning back too much . . .', 'I've got blisters on my feet . . .', 'It was wonderful . . .', 'It was excruciating . . .' Everyone, it seemed, was talking about skiing.

I soon encountered the familiar problem: going to the loo with a ski suit on! However, I was to discover that I could drink vast quantities of fluid at lunchtime but never need to go to the loo during the afternoon. I was later enlightened: at high altitudes, the body needs more fluid because the blood becomes thicker, which makes it harder for it to carry oxygen to the brain. One result is that the fluids that usually cause you to go to the loo more often – alcohol, tea, coffee – don't have that effect anymore. It certainly simplified matters.

After lunch, we moved on to *snow plough turns* – first to the right, then to the left. To do this, you must first transfer your weight to the ski in the downhill position – the one that will be on the outside of the turn – which means that you have to lean down the mountain. At the same time, you shift your centre of balance by pushing your knees in, not by thrusting out your hips or shoulders. Moving the upper body is one of the most common mistakes of novice skiers – after all, it is a natural instinct when all you want to do is hug the security of the mountainside as much as possible. To help us master this new manoeuvre, Peter told us to put our right hands on our right knees and our left arms in the air when turning to the left, and to reverse our arm positions when turning to the right.

At first, it all seemed illogical, particularly to those of us who cycle, when it is natural to lean into a turn. However, in a snow plough, what actually happens is that, by leaning out but keeping your knees pressed in, you are applying pressure to the inside

It's in all the technique . . .

For many years, different countries advocated different approaches to skiing technique. The Austrians endeavoured to minimize body movement, preferring instead to concentrate on dynamic leg action. On the other hand, in the 1930s the French under Émile Allais began to emphasize the rotation of the upper body in the execution of parallel turns. Still another technique was produced by the Professional Ski Instructors Association of America, one based on a natural body position that would lead to fluent motion.

When it became obvious that these many and various approaches were causing confusion – not least to skiing beginners – an international organization was formed

Day 2 continued

Snow plough turns

• *Do a snow plough.*
• *Transfer weight to ski that will be on outside of turn, leaning over ski and down mountain.*
• *Keep knees pressed inwards to apply pressure to inside edge of (weighted) downhill ski.*
• *Complete turn and relax.*

edge of your downhill ski and so make it turn. The joints have to act in harmony to bring about the necessary changes in weight distribution, and it is useful to imagine your body as a collection of interlinked hinges. By analysing what is happening during each manoeuvre, the action becomes more understandable and therefore easier to perform.

Once again, Liz ended up in a frustrated heap, but the award for complete incompetence went to Andy. From tentative beginnings, he would gradually pick up speed,

in an attempt to find universally accepted teaching principles. Interski – of which my friend Professor Hoppichler recently became president – held its first conference in Zürs, not far from St Anton, in 1951, and this has been repeated every four years. At the conferences, each country gives demonstrations and discusses the current state of skiing methodology.

In the Vorarlberg region of Austria, the pistes are regarded as part of the public highway system and therefore come under the jurisdiction of the police.

lose control and tumble to the bottom of the slope in a pile of splayed legs and tangled skis. I did better, but not much . . .

The class had, by now, divided into two clear groups. There were no stars at this stage, but there were two or three very slow learners who simply couldn't get the hang of it all; the rest of us were at least average and now keen to get on to some more 'real' skiing. However, as everyone developed at different speeds, there was a lot of waiting to do. On that first day, it seemed as if patience was more important than skill.

We skied more short runs, with linked snow-plough turns to both sides. Starting by skiing parallel to the mountain, straight down the fall line, we then stood up slightly, dropped into a snow plough, placed the left hand on the left knee, made a turn to the right, then skied a short distance, dropped back into the snow plough position, placed right hand on right knee and turned to the left. My body was still quite tense; Peter's comment was: 'You're skiing like an 80-year-old!' That may have been true, but at least I was still standing.

For the next half an hour, we practised making turns without using our poles, but none of us seemed to miss them. For the final routine of the day, Peter made us stand on one leg with the other ski raised vertically in front of our faces. We then put the grip-end of one pole on our foreheads, and when Peter shouted 'Ski!' we all had to shout 'Heil!' We must have resembled a herd of unicorns at a Nuremberg rally, but Peter assured us that this was really a cry for blue skies and better skiing tomorrow. It had been an exhausting day, but I had learned a lot and was still in one piece.

I deposited my equipment in Tony Pangratz's store, and experienced a glorious sensation when I finally exchanged my ski boots for my moon boots. It felt as

Faster and faster . . .

As in any sport in which speed is an integral part, there are some skiers who will go to extraordinary lengths to prove that they are the fastest.

In August 1955, an American made a bold claim: Ralph Miller swore that he had travelled at a speed of 109.14 mph over a 50-metre stretch of the Garganta Schuss at Portillo in Chile. He had been timed manually by two assistants standing half a kilometre back from the course, each clutching a stop watch. However, a little simple arithmetic will show that, to achieve that speed over that distance, Miller would have had to cover the ground in 1.0248 seconds. Because it was unlikely that the reflexes of his assistants had been quite so fast, his claim was never officially acknowledged.

Day 2 continued

if I were walking on air, and I almost floated back to the hotel. But the very best moment of the day was when I collapsed into the hotel sauna. I just lay there, surrounded by other sweating bodies, and let the things I had learned during the day sink in, before drifting off into a world of my own.

After dinner, I was ready for an early night. Actually, I was ready for an early night *before* dinner. I was so tired that I couldn't remember returning to my room. (Someone told me later that I had fallen asleep in the lift. How embarrassing . . .) When I finally got into bed, I was wafted to sleep by inner voices that told me to *'lean forward, knees in, poles back, shoulders to the . . . zzzzzzzzzz . . .'*

In 1964, Luigi di Marco set a new world speed record using a technique known as the 'caravelle', which involved him putting his head between his legs and skiing blind – a more aerodynamic position than the usual upright one.

However, when Walter Mussner tried the same technique in speed trials the following year, his inability to see where he was going caused him to crash into the timing device, and he later died of internal injuries.

Others have achieved success even while adopting a more traditional stance. For example, Portillo was again the scene when the 200-kilometre-per-hour (125 mph) barrier was breached for the first time. This staggering feat was achieved by Steve McKinney during the 1978 'Flying Kilometre'.

49

DAY 3

I again slept like a log and woke after ten hours feeling extremely virtuous and full of beans. However, when I got out of bed, I felt as if I'd been mugged by a gorilla! I hobbled about painfully as I dressed, but as I got moving, my muscles loosened up a bit and I was able to walk with minimal pain to the hotel dining room, wearing my aches and pains like invisible medals awarded me for the amazing feats I'd performed the day before!

All thoughts of heroism left me as my breakfast plate brought me down to earth. Today I felt part of the lively atmosphere. Now, like the rest of the skiers tucking into their cereal, meat, fruit and yoghurt, I was keen to get outside for my first breath of mountain air.

After breakfast, I walked briskly to the ski school, collected my skis from the store and met up with the rest of my class outside. Most people hadn't suffered too badly from the first day, although Carey had sore calves and aches in other, more tender places from falling over so much. Half of our *'Ski! Heil!'* routine of the day before had worked ed: the weather was glorious – bright blue skies and hot sun. Now all we needed was better skiing . . .

Peter strode over to where we were standing and, as enthusiastic

All aboard the sardine box . . .

There are two ways to travel up a mountainside: you can walk or, far better, you can ride up. Which method is used to transport you will vary from country to country and from resort to resort. There are cable cars, bucket lifts, chair lifts, gondolas and what are generally known simply as ski lifts, which include the T-bar. In the United States and Japan, for example, there are more chair lifts than any other kind – particularly in the latter, where the vast numbers of skiers put piste space at a premium. In Europe, on the other hand, there are more gondolas and ski lifts than there are cold, primitive and occasionally dangerous chairs.

Day 3 continued

as ever, announced, 'Yesterday was holiday. Today is *work.'*

Great, I thought. *Yesterday he promised that the first day is always the hardest!*

We began with some stretching exercises. Then we were ready for the next stage – the *sideslip*. Peter demonstrated how you place your skis across the fall line and push the edges into the snow so that you don't slide. Your upper body should be facing virtually straight down the mountain, leaning into the valley. Then, placing your poles behind you, push your knees

Although the basic cable car design – two cars attached to the same traction line – was used by the Chinese over 1000 years ago and by the Incas of South America, other types of Alpine transport are of a more recent vintage. In the 1880s an enterprising German designer built a loop ski tow to be driven by new-fangled electricity. Constructed in the Black Forest, it unfortunately failed when the available electrical power proved to be less than powerful. It wasn't until some 50 years later, in August 1934, that the Zurich engineer, Erich Konstam, took out a patent for a ski lift, and the following December, the world's first lift opened on the Bolgen slopes at Davos. It was arguably the most significant development in the sport since Sondre

down the valley so that your skis gradually come off their edges and flatten on the snow. You then start to slip sideways down the mountain, helping your movement by gently pushing the ski poles behind you.

It was a strange and awkward position, and the first time we all tried the manoeuvre, we all crashed down! Like most beginners, as soon as I started to slide my initial reaction was to lean backwards,

Sideslipping

• *Place skis across fall line.*
• *Push edges into snow.*
• *Turn upper body towards valley.*
• *Gently push knees towards valley; skis will come off edges and flatten so that you slip sideways down mountain, keeping weight mainly on downhill ski.*
• *Thrust knees into mountain to stop.*

Norheim had designed his revolutionary waisted skis almost 70 years before. Now, for the first time, skiers did not have to begin their downhill run after what was often an exhausting climb.

Two years later, in 1936, the world's first chair lift was opened in Sun Valley. This was invented by the American railway engineer, Jim Curran. During his time with the Union Pacific Railroad, Curran had constructed a number of banana-loading devices, and when he became involved in the design and construction of the Sun Valley Ski Centre, he decided that people were basically no different from the fruit he had been handling! His first designs were rejected on the grounds that they were too dangerous, but the enterprising engineer persisted

Day 3 continued

but too much of this and your skis disappear out from under you.

Ironically, we later found that the further you lean forward, the better the grip you have on the slope – even if it means that you're doing what instinct tells you is most dangerous. Of course, when Peter demonstrated how it should be done, he made it look so easy.

I found it quite hard to make a controlled descent for any distance. I managed a few sideslips in short, shuddering bursts, but I simply couldn't find a way to glide effortlessly down the hill like Peter. It was like being a tightrope walker: if he can't find the right point of balance using his pole, he may not fall, but he has to work a lot harder, leaning first one way, then the other. The idea is that, once you're in the right position and have found the correct balance between the skis' edges and their soles, you should be able to lock into that position and carry on sliding without the need for any more movement of your upper body.

To make a change, we were told to sideslip down a few feet and then thrust our knees into the mountain to bring ourselves to a sudden stop. This exercise was quite easy and made me feel

Everyone in the class was extremely supportive, and shouts of 'Good luck!' were often heard as one or other of us made another attempt. A close camaraderie had built up, and we all shared each other's elation and sympathized with each other's despair.

We spent much of the morning practising our snow-plough turns

and eventually won approval for a chair lift that was then constructed at the Idaho resort.

Like Curran, many other designers have been excited by the possibilities involved in transporting skiers up and down mountains, and the results have sometimes been extremely inventive. For example, the Territet Glion mountain railway in Switzerland incorporates a conventional two-car system but without the use of an engine to pull up the cars. Instead, once skiers have alighted from the car at the top, a reservoir in the car is filled with water and its weight sends it down the slope, simultaneously pulling up the fully laden lower car. When the water-filled car reaches the bottom, the water is jettisoned.

Day 3 continued

and sideslips, in between side-stepping laboriously up the hill to await our next turn. With Peter spending more and more time with the slower learners, some of the waiting seemed to last for ever. We all got bored, and at one point, the morale of the class reached a very low ebb. Despite Brian's urging, Liz actually dropped out and sat in the snow watching the rest of us from a vantage point higher up the slope.

A child of about four skied past, eyeing this group of incompetent adults with disbelief mixed with disdain. Young children are a delight (*and* extremely irritating) to watch on the slopes, as they fearlessly zoom around on their tiny skis. They look like cuddly toys in their padded ski suits, some

Before its collapse, the longest chair lift in the world was in Australia: the Alpine Way, which ran to the Kosciusko Chalet above Thredbo in New South Wales. Depending on the weather, it took between 45 and 75 minutes to make the 3½ mile ascent. Today, the ski lift that goes the *highest* is at Chacaltaya in Bolivia, where it rises to 16,500 feet. Travel up a further 1,019 feet and you can sample the finest Bolivian cuisine at the world's highest restaurant.

The longest gondola system is at Grindelwald-Männlichen in Switzerland, which covers 3.88 miles. Although the journey is divided into two sections, passengers remain in the same gondola throughout.

When you go abroad to ski, you may find that, although the lifts look familiar, finding out what to

Day 3 continued

with little crash helmets and over-size goggles. Fast learners, they're closer to the ground than adults and seem to bounce if they fall. Many instructors prefer to take children than teach self-conscious and rigid grown-ups. For children, learning to ski is an extension of playtime, not the seemingly humi-liating ordeal it is for their parents.

We finished the lesson with a race back to the ski school and a welcome bowl of *gulaschzuppe* at the railway restaurant. As we sped there with our poles under our arms in a racing tuck, it seemed a bit of a triumph – something none of us would have thought possible when we first began to learn to ski.

After lunch, Peter told us that we were now ready to try our first drag lift. First we had to go to the *kasse* (ticket office) to pick up our ski passes. Each of these contains a mugshot of its owner – mine, like all photo-booth portraits, made me look deranged – and you have to wear it, dangling around your neck, at all times. The Arlberg ski pass entitles you to use all the 70 or so lifts and cable cars in the region. Passes at some other re-sorts are, however, more restrict-ive, and it is a good idea to make sure that you know exactly where your pass will allow you to go *and* when it runs out.

Much to my dismay, I found that the lunch break hadn't re-freshed me as I'd thought it would. Worse, as we trudged for what seemed like miles up and down over difficult snow, I became really exhausted. This wasn't helped

call them can prove a problem. For example, in France the cable car is known as *téléferique* or *téléfrique*, while in Italy you will need to look for a *funivia*. The German-speaking nations, as logical as ever, use *luftseilbahn*, which means 'air cable railway'. Ask for a *teleferico* in Spain, while in Norway you'll need to find a *kabelbane* or *svevebane*.

The bucket lift is primarily seen in France, where it is called a *télébenne*. Colloquially it is known as the 'sardine box', which may go some way to explaining why it is so rare throughout the rest of Europe. The few bucket lifts found in Italy are called *ovovia* – literally, the 'egg route'!

In Germany and Austria, a chair lift becomes a *sessellift*, in France a *télésiège*, in Spain a *telesilla*, in Norway a *stolheis*, and in Italy a *seggiova*.

The Italians invented the canal-going gondola, so it is not surprising that they refer to the mountain version by the same name. The romantic French and Spanish refer to theirs as *télécabines* and *telecabinas* respectively, while the more stoic Germans and Norwegians prefer *gondelbahn* and *gondolheis*.

The basic ski lift retains that name in Germany, although there is another, more appealing term – the *schepplift*. In Italy, too, you will find your way by asking for a ski lift, but if you really want to impress your friends, try enquiring after the *sciovia*. In France, look for a *téléski*, and in Spain a *telesqui*. Visitors to

Day 3 continued

when we passed a small children's drag lift and Peter wouldn't let us use it. The torture of slowly side-stepping past this, which could have saved us time and a lot of effort, left me feeling very resentful. As a result, when we reached our destination – a more advanced nursery slope called the Kindlisfeld – we were all panting and thoroughly miserable.

But, here, help was at hand – a T-bar lift, a succession of upside-down Ts attached to a wire, which gently nudge the riders up the slope. Peter gave clear instructions on how to use it: take your hands out of the ski-pole straps, hold the poles in one hand on the outside of the track, place your feet slightly apart, bend your knees and press down on the front part of the skis.

'But most of all,' he said, *'don't sit down!'*

It seemed simple enough. However, after our first attempt, the scene resembled the end of a battle:

bodies strewn everywhere; poles, legs and skis jutting out from snow drifts all the way up the track. It must have been the highlight of the lift operator's day.

Peter's cries of *'Don't sit down!'* always came too late, as the next pair of skiers crashed to the ground. When someone falls, the operator has to stop the lift so that the 'debris' can be cleared. The sudden jolt as the cables took the

Norway need to ask for either a *skislep* or a *T-keis* - no prizes for guessing what the last one is . . .

Lift stations themselves can be a hazard for a number of reasons. On several occasions, particularly at the beginning, I would ski up to the queue and, finding myself unable to stop, smash into the last few

people. They were not impressed.

Ski poles, too, can become deadly weapons: as skiers converge, usually in a disorderly fashion, at the narrow entrance to a lift, it is very easy to poke out several eyes without really noticing. Because of this, poles should be held tightly in one hand with their points down.

strain often sent another two skiers flying, and progress up even that short slope was painfully slow. What happened at the top was even more hilarious than the journey there. As the bar was discarded, skiers, without a clue of what to do next, piled on top of each other like cans of fruit on a runaway conveyor belt. No, it wasn't a very impressive display from my class . . .

Once we had more or less got the hang of the T-bar, however, it was like a gift from the gods. Not only could we spend more time skiing, we were finally spared the

Swing turn

• *Ski diagonally across fall line (traversing). Keep uphill ski ahead, and downhill pole slightly in front of downhill (i.e. angling body down mountain).*
• *Push out heel of uphill ski (stemming).*
• *Plant downhill pole near tip of downhill ski.*
• *Transfer weight to stemmed ski, lean down valley and ski round pole.*
• *Bring new uphill ski parallel.*

Queuing is, of course, very much a British tradition although, to some extent, anathema to Europeans. You can always tell the British contingent at a lift station: they're the ones trying to be fair and orderly while forever becoming upset and moaning at the queue-jumping antics of the Continentals. However, this is no excuse for using poles to make kebabs of their eyes. On the other hand, some people have been known to use them to release the bindings of skiers who barge rudely in front. The easily accessible clips on the backs of modern safety bindings makes this practice easy and largely undetectable . . .

agonizing effort of sidestepping, which had already threatened to bring my short skiing career to an abrupt end.

The afternoon's lesson concentrated on developing the snow-plough turn into the basic *swing turn*. The main difference is that you start from a traverse position, heading diagonally across the mountain with your skis parallel. Then transfer your weight to the downhill ski and open (push out) the heel of the uphill ski to make half a snow plough so that you start to turn. Opening the heel of the ski in this way is called *stemming*.

As soon as possible into the turn, transfer your weight to the ski that is now downhill and bring the uphill ski parallel until you're traversing in the opposite direction. Turns are linked by stemming out the uphill ski again, transferring your weight to this, the new downhill ski, and finally bringing the skis parallel. In fact, when traversing, most of your weight should be kept on the downhill ski.

I was beginning to pick up speed and was feeling a lot more confident. However, I noticed that I was doing much better when turning from left to right, than from right to left. I thought this was strange – after all, I'm right-handed and it would seem to follow that, turning to the right, which involves co-ordination and effort through the *left* ski, would be more difficult. However, making right turns felt smooth and natural; going the other way was a completely different story.

When trying to transfer my weight correctly to go left, nothing came naturally. Peter pointed out that I was still leaning too far back – I obviously hadn't yet overcome my fear of the slope.

After spending an hour or so going up and down the Kindlisfeld practising our swing turns, a few of us formed a breakaway faction

Hannes Schneider

Skiing was not always looked upon with admiration and wonder. In 1900, the ten-year-old Austrian, Hannes Schneider, fitted with skis made from barrel staves, had to practise by moonlight to avoid the taunts and jeers of other children.

In later life, Schneider's troubles were not over. Despite combining Norheim's christiania with stemming to come up with the 'stem christie' in 1909, as well as founding the Arlberg Ski School, he was interned by the occupying Germans

in 1938 for holding 'unsympathetic views'. However, largely due to the efforts of an American called Harry Gibson, he was released and allowed to emigrate to the United States, where he lived until his death in 1954.

Speed skier, Kalevi Hakkinen, designed a special roof rack for his car so that he could practise his aerodynamic tuck while strapped to it and travelling at speed. This is now a standard training device for speed skiers.

Day 3 continued

and left the rest of the class to ski around on our own. To us, it really felt as if we'd made a breakthrough, that all the instruction was finally coming together. Our excitement was infectious.

Peter called us back for the final exercise of the day: the *kick turn*. This is used when you're in a small space, where there's no room to change direction by any other means. Peter showed us how to make a 180-degree turn to the right: first, kick the right ski into the air, as if doing the *'Ski! Heil!'* routine; plant your right pole behind you for support and your left pole by the tip of your left ski; let the right ski fall to the right, so that it's parallel with the left, but pointing in the opposite direction (for those who know ballet, this is similar to the fifth position); bring the left ski round the back of your

Kick turn

To turn 180 degrees to right:
* *Kick right ski into air and let it fall to right so it is parallel but pointing in opposite direction to left ski.*
* *Plant poles behind you at each end of uphill ski, or plant left pole by tip of uphill (left) ski and right pole below tip of downhill (right) ski.*
* *Bring left ski round back of right boot.*
* *Adjust poles so you face in opposite direction from where you started.*

Chalets

While at St Anton, I stayed at a hotel, but many skiing holidaymakers opt for chalet accommodation.

Chalets can vary in size from small apartments to something resembling mini-hotels. Some, like Carey's, are filled with a single party of friends, others by a random selection of assorted strangers. The latter variety can be a good way of making new friends, and both types allow you to share your experiences, fears and triumphs with others. While you are under no obligation to ski, dance, drink, eat or whatever with those in your chalet, if you are easily irritated by other people, you may find it all a little claustrophobic.

Many people choose to ski separately, meeting up with the others at a pre-arranged rendezvous for lunch.

Chalets are administered by tour operators, but their day-to-day running is the responsibility of the chalet girls. It is said that 'in every mountain resort, there is a piece that will be forever South Kensington...' You don't *have* to be called Harriet, Caroline, Muffy, Fiona, Lucinda, Squiffy or Fergie to be a chalet girl, but it helps.

Carey gave her chalet a glowing recommendation, praising both the atmosphere and the food. However, standards are extremely variable, especially what is placed before you at mealtimes. This may be the

Day 3 continued

right boot – it will want to unwind in that direction anyway – and adjust your poles until you're facing the opposite way from where you started.

Watching Peter, it looked like an impossible and extremely painful manoeuvre, but after a few goes, it seemed a lot more logical. The faster and more flowing you make the kick turn, the easier it becomes. The hardest part is lifting the ski to the vertical and planting it in the snow. That's when the muscles at the back of my legs came in for some punishment.

At the end of the lesson, Peter led us down the slope in a caterpillar formation. None of us could believe that we'd got this far in just two days. I was exhausted and my thoughts were firmly fixed on a sauna and bed. That would have been my choice if *I* had had any say in the matter, but I knew that I had to stay awake to film the notorious *après ski* night!

As we said our good-byes, Carey, who was staying with seven others at a chalet (*a description of chalets begins on p.61*), invited me back for a cup of good old British tea with a few of her friends. As we all tucked into an obscenely large cream cake, we discussed our impressions so far.

reasoning behind the offers of 'unlimited wine' often promised in holiday brochures. At first, this might seem like extreme generosity, but beware: unlimited wine can help to pass off a three-course meal as a four-course one, when yet another unsuccessful soufflé finds its way into the dustbin.

———

Ski clubs and resorts

Generally regarded as the oldest in the world, the Kiandra Ski Club was set up in 1861 in, of all places, Australia by a Norwegian and a group of Australian miners. It still exists today in the Snowy Mountains, although not at Kiandra, which is now uninhabited.

Day 3 continued

'The first day,' I said, 'it felt like learning to walk all over again, only using someone else's feet!'

Carey agreed. 'And did you notice how you seem to reach a barrier, when you seem to stop making progress? You know what you're supposed to do, but making it happen is another matter. I found that I got tired and depressed doing the same thing again and again and again.'

I asked the others whether they had done any exercises before coming out, and was surprised to hear that very few had bothered. My modest efforts made me feel quite virtuous.

We were interrupted by the sudden appearance of one of the other chalet residents asking one of her friends, 'Can I borrow your moon boots, Juliet?' and then in the same breath added: 'Oh, and by the way, did you know that Hugh's in hospital?'

Of the eight people staying at the chalet, four had suffered injuries, including the hapless Hugh and another who'd had to have five stitches in a head wound after falling and being hit by a wayward ski. Carey was also badly bruised, and as a result, she'd decided not to ski the next day.

'When I get back on the snow,' she said, 'I'll probably take some private lessons, to catch up any lost ground.'

I remembered what Professor Hoppichler had said, and thought that this might be a good time for me to leave the class and go for some individual tuition myself.

Carey and her friends seemed to be really enjoying chalet life. It can be an extension of your ski class, they said, with the same fun of being in a crowd. However, it wasn't one non-stop party. On the contrary, according to Carey, she and her friends rarely went out in the evening as they were normally too tired. Instead, they preferred to stay in, drink and play endless

The idea of people gathering together to ski quickly spread to Europe. During the 19th century, many of today's renowned ski resorts - for instance, Igls, Kitzbühel and Cortina - were flourishing summer resorts, famous for their healthy mountain air and invigorating hill walks. Yet, when the snows came in October, the hotels and bars shut their doors and the villages went into virtual hibernation until the spring. However, in 1864, a chance conversation between four Englishmen and Johannes Badrutt of the Kulm Hotel in the Swiss resort of St Moritz was the first step towards a massive change in the Alps.

Herr Badrutt had boasted about the magnificent weather that could be experienced at the resort in the winter, and to prove his point, he

Day 3 continued

games of Trivial Pursuit.

With only crumbs left on the plate and me wondering how many sit-ups I'd have to do as penance, I left just as Carey and her friends were settling down to yet another game. I never could remember which American state has the longest coastline anyway . . .

After I made my way back to the hotel and another wonderful sauna, I took a taxi up the mountain to a pretty little restaurant where I had arranged to meet

offered the incredulous Englishmen free accommodation. Not wishing to pass up the opportunity of an all-expenses-paid break, the visitors willingly accepted. The hotel's register shows that, that winter, 16 visitors, all from England, stayed with Herr Badrutt – in fact, they stayed for *five-and-a-half months!* St Moritz was well on its way to becoming one of today's leading re-

sorts, and others soon followed suit.

At first, skiers had to use facilities that had simply been adapted from summer to winter use. Then, in the late 1930s, the Agnelli family trust invested in a purpose-built ski centre at the Italian village of Sestrière, near Turin, which was intended for use by the employees of the Agnellis' Fiat car company. At the time it was built, it was

heavily criticized for being both extravagant and ugly, but it proved to be the model for a new generation of ski resorts that sprang up all over Europe. Like Sestrière, they aimed to provide for holidaymakers keen on getting the maximum amount of skiing out of their stay.

For most people, World War II put an end to carefree winter breaks in the Alps and elsewhere. How-ever, skiing took off in a big way in neutral Switzerland during the war years, and by the time peace was restored, the Swiss, with an esta-blished base, were prepared to launch a successful holiday indus-try. They were also helped by the fact that many soldiers who had serv-ed in Alpine regions during the war had already had some skiing experi-ence and couldn't wait for the next

Day 3 continued

some of the film crew for dinner. In the midst of good-natured joking about my skiing 'prowess', I was introduced to Pear William, a particularly lethal type of *eau-de-vie* schnapps. Skiing all day may leave you dehydrated, but four or five Pear Williams is not the ideal antidote for this.

At about 10.30, the party broke up. Duty was calling and the bright lights of the disco beckoned. I was glad that I was wearing boots with good grip soles as, apparently, I sprinted up an incline that I balked at skiing down the next day! It wouldn't have been very cool to have to be sent home with a broken leg acquired while running to reach a nightclub one drunken evening.

When we entered the disco, it was virtually deserted, and I was beginning to think that everything I'd heard about *après ski* was a myth, particularly after listening to the girls at the chalet talk about their quiet evenings in. Frankly, I couldn't really see how anyone who'd been skiing all day could stay awake to go dancing at night – I'd been ready for bed the minute my ski boots had come off. However, within an hour the disco resembled the first day of Harrods' sale, and whether it was the sauna, the loud music or the Pear William, I suddenly found that I'd got my second wind.

I was pleased to see Liz on the dance floor, beaming away, happy at last to be competing on equal terms with everyone else. The music was an odd mixture of British chart hits, Euro rock and something that sounded like speeded-up Tyrolean folk music. You could tell who the locals were – the ones singing along to the disco/ *oompah* records.

Above the dance floor was a huge screen showing videos of daring powder skiers in action – it seems that, no matter where you go in ski resorts, you're never

---

opportunity to indulge their hobby.

Today, there are about 3,200 ski resorts around the world catering for an estimated 30 million skiers. These centres are found virtually everywhere, even in some quite unlikely places. In the United States, the only state without one is (somewhat surprisingly) Texas. The entire Austrian tourist industry now revolves around skiing: for example, during the 1986/7 season (December to April) alone, the government has calculated that tourists spent 46,986,353 nights at the nation's ski resorts, a rise of 1.9 per cent over the previous year. Of these, 2,215,710 were spent by British holidaymakers.

Australia's major resort can be found at Thredbo in New South

Day 3 continued

allowed to forget the primary reason why you're there. In a funny way I felt that I too was a member of the exclusive skiers club, and I found myself imagining that it was me up there, dancing through the deep snow.

Standing near me was a young man who was obviously a ski buff. As he watched the videos, he offered a running commentary: '... That guy there, kills himself in the avalanche coming up . . . now! There you go, he's just killed himself. Did you see that?'

'Yes, thank you, I did,' I replied flatly, desperately searching for one of my classmates to rescue me from this example of a species new to me – the ski bore. Unable to find anyone I knew in the swirling activity of the dance floor, I took refuge at a table.

Eventually the day's exertions took their toll, and various members of my class and others collaps-ed into chairs around the table. The conversation, yelled above the wail of the music, revolved around skiing. Nobody seemed to be the slightest bit interested in any other aspect of life. We'd all become totally obsessed with the sport and with our own performance.

It was lovely to walk back to the hotel in the cold night air. Although it was late the streets were packed, like a scene from a Christmas card.

I was quite sad at the thought of leaving my class to go it alone. We'd become very close through our mutual suffering. However, I was keen to break through the barrier and start making some real progress. My introduction to ski lifts had been a major step forward – it had eliminated much of the drudgery that had been so much a part of the first day and a half of instruction. Now, I thought, I'm ready to go higher, steeper and faster . . .

Wales, where there is excellent skiing on the south-facing slopes of the 7,430-foot Mount Kosciusko. (Many of the runs pass through groups of gum trees.) On the other side of the globe, the main ski centre in North Africa is at the Moroccan resort of Oukaimedan in the High Atlas Mountains; lying at 8,700 feet, this was developed by the ski-loving French.

The Orient, too, is not untouched by the skiing bug. With 80 per cent of its land covered by mountains, it is not surprising that, today, Japan has one of the world's most enthusiastic skiing populations. In fact, an estimated 5-10 million Japanese use the country's 400-odd ski centres. And while a certain ski resort in South Korea may not win any prizes for its facilities, it would

certainly pick up some kind of award for possessing one of skiing's most unpronounceable names – book your holiday now for the snowy heights of Taegwallyong!

Anyone bored with the same old trip to Val d'Isère each winter might find themselves drawn to new pastures. In 1983, the *Sunday Times* contained some advice on this subject by Martin Chilver-Stainer, a former freestyle champion and something of an authority on the sport. 'There are three ski resorts in Lebanon,' he wrote. 'One is occupied by the Syrians, another by the Israelis, and in the last one, you are not advised to ski off-piste because you might stray into a minefield.'

―――

DAY 4

A lavish breakfast was out of the question – the Pear Williams had seen to that. The four (or was it five?) I'd had with the film crew had been followed by a few more at the disco and then by a quick brandy before I'd headed for bed – and I don't normally drink! As a result, this morning I wasn't feeling so good, and the last thing I wanted was a plateful of salami staring me in the face. Fruit juice would be fine, and maybe a bowl of one of the less demanding mueslis.

Although my alcoholic intake of the night before must have been more than matched by others at the hotel,* they (lucky things) seemed unaffected now. The piste maps were out again, and the day's routes were once more being frantically argued over. Skiing certainly breeds a tough following.

The first blast of mountain air bestows miraculous powers of recovery, and by the time I'd staggered to the ski school, I was more or less in full working order.

Although yesterday had been very hard work – a whole morning

*Reading through this, I find that I sound like some kind of dreadful dipsomaniac; I must stress that my heavy intake of Alpine alcohol was purely for research purposes!

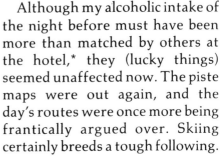

Up and away

Having become quite expert on the T-bar, I found the chair lift a new experience. The chairs - seating two and sometimes three people - are strung on an overhead cable, and swing up the mountain like a giant centipede. Skiers are funnelled past a checkpoint towards the start position, invariably floundering the last few yards to avoid the indignity of missing the chair, which comes round with alarming rapidity. It helps to ride with a friend or at least someone who won't mind being gripped as you steady yourself.

There was a clunk as a chair hit the back of our knees, and we both toppled backwards into the seat. It is probably best to be involuntary seated in this way and suffer the

of sidestepping followed by a yomp to the T-bar, then the most strenuous afternoon of skiing so far and finally a late night of drinking and dancing – I was surprised to find that I wasn't that stiff. Any slight aches were quickly walked off and I was soon fit and reasonably raring to go. I just hope that all the aches and pains that I'd expected were not being saved up to haunt me once I got home.

At the ski school, I quickly met up with my new instructor, who looked rather like a young Orson Welles plus the regulation tan and twinkle. His name was Jurgen, but he was known as 'Yogi' and I had gathered, from asking others about him the previous night, that he

bruises than to try and anticipate the chair's arrival. If your timing is out, there's a chance that you'll miss your target, land on the ground and promptly be hit in the back of the head by a flying seat. Chair lifts wait for no man (or woman).

As we swung out of the lift station, Jurgen pulled down the safety bar from above our heads so that it securely encircled us. I was pleased to see that it's impossible for the mechanism to fly open unexpectedly once your skis are on the footrest. My one fear was that, while I was negotiating my skis into position on this, I'd knock the bindings of one and release it to send it crashing to the ground below. However, although this does happen, it's very rare and is usually the result of high jinks on the chair lift.

Day 4 continued

was apparently quite a character around the village.

Almost as soon as we'd introduced ourselves, he noticed that I was carrying my skis with their tips pointing up. 'You're lucky that you haven't killed somebody already,' he commented censorious-ly. This wasn't a great beginning . . . and it didn't add to my confidence to see a group of tiny toddlers receiving their gold stars.

We were to take the mountain train to a nursery slope about 1,820 feet above St Anton. Once the barrier lifted, it was every man

My skis felt awkward as they flapped about in the air. On the snow, I had become used to having these things on my feet. Airborne, they felt cumbersome again.

The chair lift can sway quite a bit; particularly if there's a high wind; when the weather is really bad, the lift may be stopped until conditions improve. There's also a juddery moment when the chair goes over one of the supporting pylons. What with the height, the ski-flapping, the swaying and the judders, the novice's first chair-lift can be alarming.

The most noticeable thing about riding in a chair lift – and something that sets it apart from all other kinds of mountain transport – is the silence. At last, away from the chaos of the slopes and the drone of the T-bar motors, you experience a

Day 4 continued

for himself: the queue made for the train like passengers racing for the last lifeboat on the *Titanic*. Once in, bruised and battered, the carriages were jammed with drip-ing skiers holding their skis, jostling to get near the door with grim, impatient expressions on their faces. The journey was about as enjoyable as the 8.25 to Waterloo.

real sense of isolation, and I spoke to Jurgen in whispers, not wishing to upset the serenity. The mountains seemed to have been reclaimed by nature, and I was calm again.

As we approached the top, we took our skis off the foot-rest, and Jurgen lifted the safety bar. There was a frightening moment when my skis, no longer supported, lung-ed forward and threatened to tip me out of the chair, a possibility now that the safety bar was no longer there to hold me in. For a split second, I thought I was going to fall. Jurgen hurriedly told me to raise the tips of my skis, and as we drew into the upper station, they touched down and I stood up. Before I could ski away, I had to push backwards on the chair – first, to make sure that I left it behind,

73

I was just happy to look around and take in the scenery. For the first time, I really felt that I was getting up into the mountains. Admiring the spectacular views down the valley, I could see some of the more exciting runs through the forest, and it made me realize just how dull skiing on the relatively flat ground outside the school had been. *Once I've experienced some real snow,* I thought, *I'll never want to go back.* It was as if I'd learned how to drive in a car park and was now getting out on to the open road. (*Just don't go and break a leg.*)

and second, to give me enough momentum for my exit.

Jurgen said that there'd been a few cases of people staying seated while the chair went round the pulley and headed off back down the mountain. I must have looked alarmed, for he added, 'It's OK. They always stop the lift and go out to rescue them.' Thankfully, I didn't become a chair-lift statistic - at least, not this time.

Avalement **is the French word for 'swallowing'. It is used to describe a special kind of turn, but more commonly for 'swallowing up bumps': bumps are used by the skier to assist the turn.**

Day 4 continued

When we reached the top, I enjoyed some of the best views of the area that I'd seen so far, and I was much more aware of being high up. Although we were standing on a gently sloping plateau, if the unthinkable happened and I careered off down the mountain, I'd have a much longer way to fall.

There was a drag lift about 200 yards from the railway station and, as we skied towards it, Jurgen took this opportunity to gauge my prowess. I carried on from where I'd left off the day before, and was feeling competent, confident and (dare I say it?) quite stylish. He could find little fault with my performance and said that I was 'average so far'. I was pleased with myself, too, but I think Jurgen was left with the impression that I was a better skier than I actually was.

We didn't stay on the high nursery slope for very long, for once I'd convinced Jurgen that I wasn't totally useless, he decided to take me to a place called Happy Valley. On the way, I came across a whole new problem: people.

It was one of the most terrifying experiences of my life. Crowds of skiers whizzed by from all directions, and trying to make turns was like attempting to cross a busy road . . . blindfolded. People would ski up to me and, just before colliding, deftly turn away, but I didn't know they would until the very last minute. What if those speeding towards me at 40 miles an hour were as out of control as I was? They could easily crash into me and send us both hurtling down the mountain. I really do think that someone should introduce a system of skiing L-plates for beginners; then faster skiers could try to avoid them. As it was, my experience on that slope was like a game of Russian roulette – only the odds weren't as good.

Luckily, I was involved in only one collision, with an Austrian

Sondre Norheim

When the Olympic flame for both the 1952 and the 1960 winter games was lit at a simple cottage in Morgedal in the Telemark district of southern Norway, skiers were honouring the memory of the man who had been born there in 1825: Sondre Norheim. Basically a simple man, but highly imaginative and very good with his hands, Norheim built the first pair of waisted skis (which were narrower in the middle than at the tips and heels and made turning easier and more controllable); these incorporated a set of bindings. The result was a revolution in the capability of the skier.

Before his death in 1897, the inventive Norwegian also developed

Day 4 continued

woman. I am positive that it was more her fault than mine; I just happened to stop in an inconvenient place. After we'd both picked ourselves up and brushed off the snow, she became quite abusive, rattling off insults in German. The only phrase I knew in the language was *'Gehen wir zusammen ins Kino?'* which means 'Shall we go to the cinema together?' I couldn't think of anything better to say in the circumstances, so I gave it a try. It didn't exactly work: she stuck out her tongue at me. I wished I'd never asked.

Compared to the short, repetitive exercises we'd done on the nursery slopes, making a real journey on skis was very different. In the nurseries, provided you didn't fall, each run would be over in less than a minute, from setting off at the top of the T-bar to joining the queue back at the lift station. Now we were actually going somewhere, using our skis as transport.

I soon discovered that there was only one way to get down, and that was on skis. However much I may have wanted to give up – and I often did – I couldn't. On the mountain, there's no alternative but to keep going. Jurgen spurred me on by saying that skiing down is always the quickest way. This encouraged me, particularly at my very low points.

I now encountered much steeper slopes than I had before, and the unfamiliarity of the run really kept me alert. Back on the nursery slopes, the repetitiveness meant that I became very familiar with the terrain and soon learned the easiest routes over the best snow. There, I would discover, usually by coming to grief, where the treacherous bits lay and was able to steer well clear of them on subsequent runs. Then, all I had to concentrate on was improving my technique, but now, in addition to remembering how to stay on my feet, I had to be much more aware

two of today's basic skiing manoeuvres. The first was the sweeping turn that he accomplished on his waisted skis, and which became known as the 'Telemark', after his home district. The second was the basic parallel swing that he named after Christiania, the former name of Norway's capital Oslo, and which later became incorporated with stemming to become the well-known 'stem christies'.

Kitzbühel is to ski racing what Wimbledon is to tennis and Lords is to cricket.

of what was happening underfoot, as well as looking ahead of me to see where I was going and to the sides to keep clear of human hazards.

There was a lot to think about, and my face must have shown signs of deep concentration, mixed with more than a hint of fear. I began to wish that I hadn't impressed Jurgen quite so much first thing – if I hadn't, we might still be pottering up and down the nursery slopes, enjoying the pretty views over the valley. Still, Jurgen was very good. He didn't force the

Going for gold

The world of competitive skiing encompasses many varieties of the sport, including downhill racing, the slalom, giant slalom, ski jumping, cross-country and freestyle.

A French journalist from Alsace was the driving force behind the combining of various skiing events into the World Cup as it is known today. Serge Lang modelled his system on the one used in Grand Prix motor racing – that is, competitors accumulate points from a series of events, comprising downhill, slalom and giant slalom, throughout the season. There are individual titles for each of these – for example, Valeri Tzyganov became the first Soviet skier to win one when he took the World Cup downhill title at

Day 4 continued

pace, and whenever I wanted a rest, he was happy to let me take one.

These frequent pauses during the lesson gave me a chance to look around. For an area that looked so wild and inhospitable from the air, at ground level there was overwhelming evidence of man's presence. The whole mountain range, it seemed, had been carved up and developed for the use of skiers.

The areas of piste were marked by distinctive red, green and white boundary balloons, and there were other coloured signposts indicating the numbers and classifications of the runs. Green ones are the easiest. Intermediate skiers spend most of their time on a mixture of blue and red runs. Domain of the advanced skiers – and often only the bold ones at that – are the black runs, which are usually marked on piste maps as short, straight lines running down from the

region's highest mountains. On the other hand, the map markings for blue runs wiggle a bit more, as do the skiers you find on them.

As I looked about, chair lifts seemed to soar from every direction and cable car pylons jutted out from the mountain, high into the sky. Above my head, bright yellow 'gondolas' drifted slowly by, transporting yet another cargo of skiers to the higher slopes. These strange, brightly coloured bubbles, which are just big enough to hold four people and their equipment, are becoming one of Alpine Europe's most common forms of transport, and provide a much more civilized and leisurely ride than the overcrowded cable cars, which often carry up to 100 people at a time.

Colourful warning signs for vehicle routes, hazards and closed areas littered the mountainside like discarded lollipops, and on some of the runs, bridges had

Aspen, Colorado during the 1981/2 season - and the points gained in all three go towards the skier's overall World Cup total.

The system initially favoured good all-rounders, but as skiers became more specialized, the balance gradually tipped in favour of the slalom skiers. This became even more marked in 1971 when the programme was increased from 17 to 31 events. From then on, downhillers found it increasingly hard to collect enough points from the slalom events to achieve respectable overall World Cup ratings, and as a result, the World Cup has become the sole preserve of brilliant slalom skiers such as Gustavo Thöeni, Phil Mahre and the legendary Swede, Ingemar Stenmark.

Nevertheless, the downhillers

still retain their prestige and their glamour - who but Robert Redford could have played the hero in the film *Downhill Racer*? - and they face many exhilarating challenges throughout the world. For instance, the longest downhill race in the world is the 'Inferno', which takes place at Mürren in Switzerland, the course measuring 8.7 miles from the top of the Schilthorn to Lauter-brunnen. In this or any other race, it is a disadvantage to go first or last. The course performs better once it has been skied a few times, but by the end of the day, it will have deteriorated, carved up by the tracks and grooves left by many skis.

An unfortunate misunderstanding during the Olympic downhill at Squaw Valley in 1960 probably

Day 4 continued

been built to carry skiers over a crevasse or a sudden drop. At times, the mountain seemed to be as finely prepared as the cricket pitch at Lords, and with all the other paraphernalia and people, there were times when I felt as if I were driving round Piccadilly Circus, not skiing in the supposed wilderness of the Alps. I began to appreciate why 'powder skiers' are so drawn to areas far from the piste. Only there can they escape from the turmoil of a busy blue run, crammed solid with hesitant beginners and impatient experts, each a danger to the other.

However, my immediate problem was staying upright and out of trouble; I could worry about this other, more philosophical aspect of the sport later. Jurgen was proving to be as unreliable in his reassurance as Peter had been. After I'd tumbled down what seemed like an almost sheer face, Jurgen promised me that the worst part was now over and that we were nearly there. Fifteen minutes later, I tumbled down an equally, if not more difficult, face. Imagine my confusion when he told me that this was, in fact, the trickiest bit and that we were still 'nearly there'. Still, I suppose that it doesn't really matter, as long as you believe your instructor at the time. By taking his or her word, albeit against your better judgement, you somehow find the resolve to go on.

We finally arrived at a chair lift, and I must confess to having mixed feelings. On the one hand, I was thrilled to have got this far and was now grateful to be able to rest, but on the other, I was a bit distressed to see that we were going up higher again. *Why can't we carry on down to the ski school?* I pleaded silently. *Aren't we just making more work for ourselves?*

Having survived the chair lift off we went again and Jurgen

changed the course of skiing history. The French team had posted their former champion Émile Allais, armed with a stop watch, halfway down the course, his task being to inform members of the team of their times as they passed him. He was told to crouch if the skier was behind, and to stand up straight if the competitor was in front.

As Jean Vuarnet came by, the stop watch showed that the Frenchman was a fraction of a second slower than the leader, Hans Peter Lanig. Allais crouched down low to inform Vuarnet, who then found new resolve and skied as he had never done before. At the end of the run, the flying Frenchman had taken the lead.

Next down was French hero Adrien Duvillard, who had been predicted to take the gold. As he approached Allais with a two-second lead, the latter bent down to get a better view, but Duvillard interpreted this as a signal that he was behind. He tried to raise his performance, but bemused by Allais's behaviour, he momentarily lost his concentration, caught a large bump and fell. Team mate Vuarnet emerged the victor.

In downhill racing, it is permissible to finish on only one ski or with only a single pole. For example, in 1982, Austria's Erwin Resch won the bronze medal at the World Championships at Schladming despite losing a pole during one of his runs. However, attempting to finish without either skis or poles will usually result in instant disqualification . . .

Schussing

Probably the first manoeuvre carried out in anger by a beginner, schussing - from the German word for 'shot' - simply means skiing straight down the fall line with skis together. As you are skiing downwards in a straight line, you pick up maximum speed, and speed skiers schuss in a tucked position for the fastest times. Beginners, however, should just let go and let gravity do the rest. *A word of warning*: it is important to learn how to stop before schussing too fast!

Day 4 continued

asked me to stay in his tracks, but as my concentration began to flag, I found this more and more difficult, and soon I was choosing my own way.

We reached a section of the piste that resembled a motorway – an invitation for the slow to go fast and the fast to go even faster. The only consolation was that at least everyone was going in the same direction. Jurgen pulled down his goggles and gave me an almighty shove in the back, as if to say: 'Catch me if you can!' Well, if you can't beat 'em, join 'em.

I followed in a racing tuck, crouching low with my poles squeezed under my arms. Suddenly, the air, which had seemed so warm before, became a cold wind on my cheeks. The sensation of going as fast as I could was tremendously exciting, and I didn't feel any fear or unsteadiness. I wanted to shout with delight, and I probably did.

Finally we reached our destination, one of the many *hüttes* dotted around the mountain. I was shattered, worn out from my exertions and also mentally drained from having to concentrate so hard on my technique while, at the same time, remaining aware of everything going on around me. However, I had a great feeling of accomplishment and was very proud of myself for making it from A to B in one piece. The falls I'd had along the way now seemed like occupational hazards and were easily forgotten. Jurgen was very complimentary, saying that I had done very well to complete that run after only three days of instruction. He said all the right things.

A *hütte* is basically a bar perched on the mountainside, either an old converted farm hut or one specially built in the traditional style. *Hüttes* are staffed by locals dressed in *lederhosen* and hats with feathers

Top races are often decided by tenths of a second and sometimes by much less. For instance, at the 1980 Winter Olympics, Thomas Wassberg of Sweden won the gold medal in the 15-kilometre cross-country race by a mere *one-hundredth* of a second. After a race lasting 41 minutes 57.63 seconds, Wassberg nudged the unfortunate Finn, Juha Mieto, into second place. place.

Given these narrow victories, it says a lot for the achievements of the Austrian Toni Sailer who, at the 1956 Olympics in Cortina, won the giant slalom by a massive margin of 6.2 seconds. He went on to win the slalom by 4 seconds and the downhill by 3.5 seconds, in one of sport's most outstanding personal performances. The fame he received for this achievement led to a film

Day 4 continued

Day 4 continued

stuck in the hatband, and skiers can walk on the bare wooden floorboards in their ski boots after leaving their skis outside. They serve beer, schnapps and *glühwein*, a red, fruity and warming mulled wine (*glühwein* means 'glowing wine'), as well as a simple menu.

I had become quite good at ordering bowls of *gulaschzuppe*, and was now able to ask a native to come with me to the cinema and then go for a bowl of goulash soup. The world was my oyster.

In the afternoon, Jurgen worked on the finer points of my technique, starting with my traversing position. Traversing is one of the most fundamental skills in skiing, and beginners will spend much of their time linking swing turns with long traverses.

I hadn't improved much since my lessons with Peter, and my main fault was still the fact that I leaned back into the hill. Jurgen tried to help by adjusting other parts of my body. By correcting these, he hoped to make it impossible for me to do anything except lean *away* from the mountain.

The uphill ski should lead the downhill one at all times. For me, this was quite natural when I was traversing to the left, but not so

contract, but he was allowed to continue racing as long as he was not seen to be making money from skiing. The producers reckoned that his draw at the box office would still be impressive despite roles in which he abandoned skis for shoes. They may have been right: in a nationwide poll to find the man who had done most for Austria, Sailer came fifth, behind Mozart.

While his skiing continued to shine – he won two more golds and a silver at the 1958 World Championships – his cinematic star did not, Sailer's career in the movies being as unremarkable as his prowess on the slopes was memorable. Ironically, it was not his acting that put an end to his hopes of defending his Olympic titles: a ruling over receiving money for an endorse-

Day 4 continued

easy going the other way. If the uphill ski is behind, stemming becomes more difficult, and there is the added danger that the ski tips will cross: as you transfer your weight to the stemmed ski (which then becomes the new downhill ski), it is possible to trap the uphill ski under the tip of the stemmed one. This usually happens just when you need it to be free so that you can bring it back parallel with the other one.

If your uphill ski is leading, it follows that your ankles, your knees and (it is hoped) your hips are angled away from the mountain – the basis of a good traversing posture. My problem wasn't in the knees and ankles, but making an inward swivel from the hips upward. Ideally, this part of the body should lean into the valley even more than the knees and ankles.

However, posture is something you ultimately have to sort out yourself. It's all very well having instructions bawled at you as you're coming down a mountain, but after a while, the words just seem to go in one ear and out the other, particularly if you're tired.

There is one way that you can get a good indication of how you're standing: look at the position of your poles. They should be held out in front and slightly to one side. If your downhill arm is ahead, your shoulders are probably angled too much into the mountain. By correcting the position of your arms and shoulders, you can go some way towards achieving a good traversing posture without having to think about leaning down the mountain. In this way, you can painlessly overcome a difficult barrier.

I was also rushing my turns – that is, not completing them smoothly and with control. There was a point, halfway through the manoeuvre, when I would cross the fall line and pick up speed. In

ment led to Sailer being barred from the 1960 Olympics. His appeal with audiences also suffered as a result, and today he runs the junior ski school at Kitzbühel.

Unlike Toni Sailer, some competitive skiers never receive the acclaim they deserve. In the 1952 Olympic Games in Oslo, 20-year-old Austrian prodigy Anderl Molt-

erer was included in the national team as a reserve for the downhill event – basically, it was argued, for the experience. He was asked to ski the course as a forerunner, and his time was recorded but not published. Imagine his chagrin when it became known to a select few that his time would have won him the gold medal had he been given the

the panic of the moment, I'd bend my knees, lean back and skid, rather than steer round the corner. I'd then lift my uphill ski off the snow as I brought it back parallel, and at my crisis point, my whole weight was on the downhill ski.

Jurgen showed me how it should be done. I watched as he slid his skis together effortlessly, seemingly with all the time in the world. 'If you lean forward,' he said, 'the extra weight on the front of your skis will keep them in contact with the snow. That will give you more control.' Leaning forward seemed to be the answer for everything.

It's also important to choose a good place at which to start a turn. Through constantly being skied, most runs become lower in the middle than at the sides, so we made wide sweeps and stemmed at the highest comfortable point near the edge. When we moved on to undulating terrain, Jurgen made his turns on the tops of bumps, using the upward incline to slow him down and the downward slope to accelerate away. He tried to drill a rhythm into me: traverse, stem, plant the pole, round the pole, parallel, traverse and so on.

chance to compete! Despite going on to become an exceptional racer, throughout his career Molterer never won an Olympic or World Championship gold.

All these racers lived and breathed skiing, but one man did recognize that the competitive spirit can also be present in those who cannot devote their lives to the sport.

Arnold Lunn, who was to become the first 'ski knight' when he was honoured by the Queen in 1952, devised a race open only to skiers who lived too far from the mountains to ski daily or whose jobs allowed them to ski only at weekends. The first race for the Duke of Kent Cup was in 1937, the events later becoming known as the Citadin Races.

Day 4 continued

After planting his pole, Jurgen would slightly *unweight* his skis before skiing round it, so that it looked like he was making a little jump. This 'unweighting' is an important principle and one that becomes particularly relevant when beginners move on to parallel turns. It basically involves moving the body to reduce the weight on the skis.

If that sounds impossible, try an experiment on your bathroom scales. Stand on them and bend your knees. Then thrust your body upwards from the knees, keeping your feet firmly in contact with the scales. You'll notice that you become light for a moment, and if you use this technique on the snow, your skis will become easier to turn as the weight on them is

Switzerland's Erika Schinegger first came to the world's attention when she won the downhill at the 1966 World Championships. However, with many expecting great things from her in the 1968 Olympics at Grenoble, her mother announced that Erika was in hospital recovering from an operation and would be unable to compete, but she hoped to return to the slopes in time for the 1970 World Championships. Erika did return, but as *Eric* Schinegger and with the ambition of winning the *men's* downhill title. Eric never equalled Erika's success, and was unable to achieve the unique double.

Day 4 continued

reduced. While still on your scales, try dropping suddenly in a crouch; you will see how you become momentarily heavier.

Jurgen then got me to try a few new exercises to break up the run. While traversing, I first lifted my uphill ski off the snow and skied on one leg. This was relatively easy since I had been carrying most of my weight on the downhill ski for some time now. However, lifting my downhill ski was a lot more difficult, and I found that I could only balance for a second or two at a time.

He then asked me to traverse and kick both ankles downhill to produce a small sideslip, then to relax and slide back into the traverse. Mastering the sideslip is one of the most important skills in skiing as, at the end of a swing turn, it has to be used to control your speed. I had already discovered the point of acceleration as you cross the fall line, but I was not

very good at dealing with it. For the apprehensive beginner, the sideslip is also the only effective way of getting down very narrow, steep or icy slopes. Sometimes I wished that there were steps, but I suppose that would have taken the fun out of it . . .

Finally, I was introduced to the *garland*, which is a variation of the swing turn. You begin by traversing and opening the uphill ski as if making a normal stem turn. However, as you begin to accelerate down the fall line, you bring the stemmed ski parallel with a side-slipping movement, so that you

Freestyle skiing

Although it has its origins much further back in skiing history, free-style really took off in the early 1960s, when an American, Doug Pfeiffer, established his 'School of Exotic Skiing'. By 1970, an under-ground movement had emerged and the term 'hot dogging' was born, which some say was borrowed from surfing, while others claim that it was coined on the slopes.

At first, there were few rules governing freestyle events, and competitors became increasingly daring, urged on by huge crowds, eager for bigger and bigger thrills. Then the inevitable happened: two skiers were left permanently para-lysed after horrific accidents. This led to the formation of, in 1974, the

International Freestyle Skiers' Association and, the following year, the European Freestyle Skiers' Association, both of which aimed to place controls on the sport to reduce injuries and to give it respectability.

One of the great things about freestyle is that it can be enjoyed in some degree by even the most casual skier. While many of the front and back flips seem to combine Olympic-standard gymnastics with advanced aeronautics, other figures are simple, easily learned and every bit as exhilarating. There are three main divisions: bumps, ballet and aerial.

Bumps, or moguls, are formed in the snow by skiers carving the mountainside, and are accentuated by subsequent snowfalls, turning a

Day 4 continued

Because the garland involves short swings, I was able to build up quite a satisfying rhythm. In fact, as soon as you start to appreciate the rhythm of skiing, it becomes a lot more exciting. You become mesmerized by your movement, and the whole experience is quite sensual.

We went on to make our stems narrower and our turns shorter, and I was really beginning to enjoy myself. However, without the respite of a long traverse between turns, the constant effort was very tiring. From time to time, I'd fail to move my ski or to change my weight quickly enough, and I'd find myself heading out of control towards the side of the track. Jurgen would pick me up, make sure that I was all right and invariably assure me that we were 'nearly there'.

end up heading in the same direction as your original traverse. You'll notice that you haven't actually crossed the fall line and, in effect, have completed a half turn and a sideslip. This is an excellent way to lose height if there isn't enough room to make a series of fully linked traverses.

There's no doubt that private instruction is a good way to improve your technique quickly.

once relatively flat area into an undulating field. The freestyle bump skier attempts to ski through mogul fields in the most spectacular way possible, incorporating jumps and other manoeuvres.

Ballet is to skiing what Torvill & Dean are to skating. Tricks and routines are choreographed to music with an emphasis on smoothness and originality.

• The Royal Turn has the skier gliding on one ski with the other raised behind and to the side.
• The Charleston is like the dance, but it is easier to accomplish on the dance floor than on snow.
• In the Mermaid, the skier glides on one ski while the other is raised to touch the head, which is arched back.
• The Worm Turn is a tumbling manoeuvre: while schussing, the

Day 4 continued

In a class, you'll never receive the kind of attention that you do on a one-to-one basis, particularly (and ironically) if you are of average ability and not in desperate need of constant tuition. I did miss the

fun of being part of a group, though, and occasionally found myself wondering how my former companions were getting on. I also didn't have anyone else around to make me look good and give me confidence. With Jurgen, I was definitely bottom of a class of two and was left feeling pretty hopeless most of the time.

As we finally approached the ski school, Jurgen looked back and pointed to a figure halfway up the mountain. The object of his attention was a skier dressed in old-fashioned breeches, socks and a woolly hat, who was doing what Jurgen explained was a 'Telemark turn'. This is one of the oldest types of skiing turns and was invented by one of the sport's greatest innovators, Sondre Norheim.

The Telemark is a long sweeping turn, and involves one ski being thrust forward in front of the other. The skier above us almost knelt on his rear ski as he glided

performer sits down on the back of the skis, then rolls over to one side, folding the legs and keeping the skis tight to the back. He continues to roll until the ski soles are flat on the snow, when he rises and continues.
• The Wong Banger (named after gymnast Wayne Wong) involves planting the poles on each side and then kicking up and over to make a full somersault between the poles,

to land you on your feet again.
• A Doughnut incorporates a 360-degree turn, using the skier's buttocks as the pivot.
Aerial skiing is the most spectacular form of freestyle, although far more care about safety is now taken than before. The range of figures that can be performed in the air is almost limitless, but the following are some of the most common:

around in a long arc, but he was only able to do this because his boots and bindings were much more flexible than modern equipment. It was refreshing to see someone skiing so differently from everybody else, and the Telemark skier also looked a lot more graceful than the frantic modern downhillers around him.

Jurgen and I chatted as we headed towards Tony Pangratz's equipment store, and I told him about what I'd seen of the area so far. He was not impressed with my sampling of St Anton's eateries and suggested that, for dinner, he would take me to a long-established restaurant he knew that was set deep in the heart of the forest. I agreed, and we made arrangements to meet later at my hotel.

When I finally got back there, exhilarated by my achievements during the day, I met up with Joanne as both of us were about to dive into a well-earned sauna. She said that it had been a good day for

• In the Backscratcher, the heels of the skis are brought up to touch the skier's back. Two variations are the Star, in which the skis are held together at the heels but pushed apart at the tips, and the Iron Cross, in which the skis are crossed.

• The Spread Eagle, in which the legs and arms are thrust apart, is the most straightforward of aerial figures, and one achieved involuntarily by many out-of-control piste bashers!

• In the Daffy, the legs are pushed apart in the direction of travel so that it looks as if the skier is taking a giant footstep in the air. If a number of Daffies are performed in a row, this is called a Space Walk.

Day 4 continued

the class, too, and everybody felt that they'd made progress. We'd all tasted real skiing at last.

As I went to open the door of the sauna, two naked men burst out and rushed past us shouting: '*Schnee! Schnee!*' Joanne and I watched in stunned silence as they threw open the hotel door and dived headlong into the snow outside. They proceeded to roll about in the snow, screaming deliriously, right under the window of the hotel restaurant. Inside, the diners hardly batted an eyelid and seemed more interested in the veal escalope than the spectacle outside.

After a while, the two men stood up and, with a look of satisfaction on their faces and a healthy colour on their cheeks (*all* their cheeks), sauntered back inside. As they passed the two of us, they nodded and calmly said: '*Guten Abend.*' I contemplated asking them whether they would like to go to the cinema with me, but thought better of it: they might think me a bit forward . . .

In the evening, Jurgen drove me to the restaurant down miles of winding mountain roads. These were banked on each side by huge snow drifts, but the car's snow chains gave us a good grip and we sped through the narrow lanes as if we were taking part in a 24-hour rally. Luckily, no one came along in the opposite direction.

The restaurant itself was the most 'olde worlde' and traditionally Tyrolean that I'd been to so far. The wooden building looked like something straight out of the pages of *Heidi*. Once again, schnapps was the order of the day. In British restaurants, you first get a menu; in Austria, you get a Pear William shoved in front of you as soon as you sit down at your table. It certainly warms you up.

Over our meal, we discussed the day's skiing and my progress. 'You must try to concentrate on leaning

A study carried out by the German Ski Association suggested that the main offenders against the code of ski discipline were the French, Italians and Germans, although not necessarily in that order. The best-behaved skiers, according to the report, were the British and Americans.

The American-devised Graduated Length Method and the French *ski évolutif* developed as teaching methods almost simultaneously. Both advocate the use of short-learning skis that are safer and easier to turn. GLM starts with one-metre skis that increase in three stages to equal the skier's height.

Day 4 continued

down the hill,' Jurgen said. 'Everything else will fall into place if only you'd improve your posture.'

However, he went on to say that I'd made a very good effort, considering it was only my third day. Tomorrow we'd go to a place called Rendl Beach where, he promised, he'd work really hard to turn me into an expert skier.

It sounded terrifying – time for another schnapps . . .

The 1936 Olympics

Almost all the modern Olympics have been embroiled in some political issue, and the 1936 winter games at Garmisch-Partenkirchen in Nazi Germany were no exception.

During the opening ceremony, the British team were told to make a clear Olympic salute - with one arm out to the side - as they passed in front of Hitler, so that the gesture could not be confused with the Nazi variety. One member of the team did this so enthusiastically that she hit the young woman standing next to her on the nose! The trouble the team took to differentiate between the games' salutation and a *'Heil, Hitler!'* came to nothing, however, as the radio commentator announced provocatively, 'The British are greeting the Führer with a German salute.'

One member of the German team was Gustav 'Guzzi' Lantschner. He had represented Austria in many world championship races in the past, but having become a Nazi, he now switched his allegiance to the Third Reich. As a result, and despite winning a silver medal in the combined Alpine event, he was greeted by howls of derision from the Austrian section of the crowd.

The Garmisch-Partenkirchen games were not, however, all doom and gloom. In particular, Diana Gordon-Lennox of Canada attracted a great deal of attention from the press. This was not because of her performance - she came 32nd in the downhill and second from last in the slalom - but because she competed with one arm in a sling and wearing a monocle!

An Englishman called W. D. 'Bill' Edlin employed local youths to repair the worst holes and ruts that appeared in the Parsenn-Küblis run, above Davos in Switzerland. Edlin, who became known as the 'Father of Parsenn', was rumoured to have paid the young helpers out of his own pocket. From these humble beginnings was formed the Parsenn Patrol, which became the model for ski patrols all over the world.

DAY 5

Like the morning before, I woke to hardly any stiffness at all. It was a beautiful day, the best so far, with clear blue skies and blazing hot sunshine. When I met up with Jurgen, he reminded me that we were going to Rendl Beach. With weather like this, it sounded just the place for me. However, I somehow knew that Jurgen's idea of a beach was bound to be different to mine.

We stored our skis in racks on the outside of one of the brightly coloured gondolas, and then stepped inside. As the little pod swung up the mountain, there was time to chat and take in the scenery. We were floating over a part of the region that I hadn't seen before, and the views were truly amazing. Inside the gondola, there was almost the same feeling of peace that I'd found on the chair lift, and if it had been a cold and windy day, it certainly would've been a much more comfortable ride than in an exposed chair.

After quite a long journey, we disembarked at the top station and feasted our eyes on the sights and sounds of Rendl Beach. It was a bowl of pure white snow – a perfect sun trap. I don't think I've ever experienced such intense brightness. Outside the obligatory *hütte*, the Alpine sun worshippers were already firmly established in rows of deckchairs. Below a cool array of sunglasses, one-piece ski suits were opened to the waist, revealing a vast assortment of brightly coloured T-shirts, and there were even some bikinis. Noses, cheeks and foreheads had been protected with blobs of melting sun-tan cream.

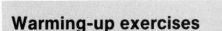

Warming-up exercises

In addition to any preparatory exercises you might have done before your holiday (or wish you had), it is a good idea to start each ski session with a few on-snow warming-up exercises. Most of the ones that Jurgen showed me involve stretching, and there's no strenuous workout designed to build up strength or stamina. However, you may find that skis can be useful pieces of fitness apparatus, either as weights or supports.

First, Jurgen kicked one ski into the air and planted the heel in the snow, as if about to do the '*Ski! Heil!*' routine. He then leaned forward and touched his forehead on

the outstretched leg, at the same time rocking gently up and down from the waist. He repeated the procedure with the other leg. When I tried this, I could really feel the muscles pulling at the backs of my knees.

Then with both skis on the ground, and using his poles for support, he pushed one leg back as far as it would go; then he repeated it with the other leg. This stretches the calf and top-of-the-thigh muscles.

Jurgen finished the sequence with two other simple exercises: bending forward from the waist; and lifting alternate skis off the ground in the same way that Peter had shown us on the first day.

Day 5 continued

It is impossible to over-emphasize just how important it is to be adequately protected from the sun in this thin air. The average British tourist is used to the more diffuse rays of our summer sun, and is often burned to a cinder after only a couple of days in the Alps. And you should put your sunscreen on *all* exposed skin: because the sunlight is reflected off the snow in all directions, parts that would not be affected by the sun on a beach can become painfully burned on the slopes. Don't forget to use it even on cloudy days – the ultraviolet rays that cause burning can penetrate gloomy skies.

My experience outside the sauna the night before still loomed large, so I was cheered when Jurgen immediately led me into the bar for a 'livener'. Having eased my way into the day on muesli and orange juice, a *glühwein* at 9.30 a.m. seemed over the top, but who was I to argue?

As we sat at the bar soaking up the sun, the last thing I wanted to do was ski. We were brought back to earth by a chap on the other side of the terrace who'd obviously recognized me and began giggling with his friends. Then he walked over to us and asked if he could have my autograph. To my surprise, he ripped open his ski suit to reveal his T-shirt – and a picture of 'Wicked Willy' confronted me! Now, I'd never signed a willy before, but doing *Treasure Hunt* helps you cope with all kinds of unexpected situations . . .

Jurgen decided that it was time for us to go and do some skiing. I reluctantly gave up my seat, swigged back the last drop of *glühwein* and went to collect my skis and my wits.

I'd mentioned to Jurgen that I had done a number of simple exercises at home to prepare myself for skiing. He said that that was a sensible thing to do.

Snow

Snow is an ever-changing and greatly variable medium. Each of its most basic units - snow flakes -is unique and, when seen under a microscope, incredibly delicate and extremely beautiful. In fact, the mathematician/astronomer who, in 1611, wrote the first serious study of snow, entitled it *The Six-cornered Snow Flake; an ideal gift for a mathematician for it comes from heaven and looks like a star.*

If you're just learning how to ski and having to spend many hours on well-prepared pistes, you'll be unable to take part in the hearty stories of 'exhilarating powder' until much later in your skiing career.

However, you'll soon come to appreciate how even the same slope can behave quite differently on successive days. Your feet will tell you about the snow's speed and turning characteristics, while your ears will supply further information gleaned from the sound underfoot. You'll encounter heavy and dry snow as well as bumps and ice, all of which can be identified by your newly educated feet and ears.

The Austrian teaching method places great importance on the skier's ability to adapt to the different types of surface, one of its primary aims being to produce the 'compleat' skier, as happy on hard pistes as in deep powder. The following are some of the conditions

with which you should be familiar:
• *Heavy wet snow* Deep, mushy snow produced after a thaw. As well as being unpleasant to ski on, extra effort is required to carry out all manoeuvres.
• *Breakable crust* Formed when the surface melts and then refreezes. The resulting hard top layer may not be strong enough to support your weight. Slopes facing the morning sun sometimes form a breakable crust in the late afternoon, when hot sunlight gives way to falling temperatures.
• *Ice* Most likely to occur on unprepared slopes, particularly those facing the sun. Busy pistes can also be polished into an icy surface. It's difficult to edge efficiently on ice, and for this reason, it's best avoided whenever possible.

100

Day 5 continued

Now we were ready to go skiing. We practised some turns, and Jurgen said that I should concentrate on making sure that I completed the manoeuvre properly; I was still rushing and losing control at the end. I soon began to wish that I'd never left my deckchair: everything I thought I'd learned up to now seemed to desert me. I felt as useless as if it were my first hour on skis, not my fourth day of tuition. To say this was demoralizing would be an understatement. It was such a shame, too, because it was the nicest day and the most beautiful setting.

My performance was humiliating. Jurgen tried to get me to sideslip and then traverse while lifting the inside ski. On both counts, I let him down badly and myself down painfully. At almost every turn, I either leaned the wrong way or got my feet into the wrong position. The net result was always the same: an unglamorous crash to the ground. After the ninth or tenth time, I began to get very angry with myself, beat the snow with my fists and then again apologized at great length to my long-suffering instructor. The more I tried to apply myself, the worse I seemed to get.

It didn't help that there was a lot of ice around, which even for a good skier is more difficult to cope with than a friendly, well-surfaced piste. Nevertheless, I wouldn't want to use that as an excuse. I was skiing badly, although exactly *why* was something of a mystery.

Struggle on, I thought. *It can only get better, and anyway, it isn't that long until lunch.*

Jurgen concentrated on my sideslipping which, he repeated, was an important technique to master, but one that most beginners found extremely difficult. He added that most people have a mental block

---

• *Rutted frozen snow* Often found in the spring after a hot day's skiing on granular snow. As the temperature falls in the late afternoon, ridges made by skis freeze into hard ruts.

• *Wind-formed snow* High winds drive the surface into waves of hard snow. Extra care is needed to prevent ski tips being caught in the crests of these snow waves.

• *Wind slab* Formed by a build-up of hard snow masses that have been compacted by the wind, and usually occurring on lee slopes after a storm. Areas where wind slab are found are often extremely unstable: blocks of snow may break off while they're being skied over. At best, wind slab is difficult to ski on; at worst, it's a potentially lethal avalanche hazard.

• *Powder snow* Fresh snow containing a high percentage of air, and which hasn't been compacted. This is a source of much skiing mythology. While advanced skiers boldly set out to find untouched slopes, beginners must be content to sit in the hotel bar and listen to the lengthy *après ski* accounts of the 'powder experience', and dream of one day having enough skill to discover these magical territories for themselves. When that day arrives, however, they'll have to concentrate, for the thrill of being waist deep in frothy white powder, trail blazing with a series of exaggerated jump turns, is often tempered by the knowledge that it can have a treacherous base. Under the surface lurk bumps and hollows, rocks and ridges, all of which can

Day 5 continued

about the manoeuvre, but when they get over it, they see how easy it really is. I hoped he was right and not just trying to make me feel better.

Today's attempts at sideslipping could more accurately have been described as 'side-juddering'. My skis seems to have a mind of their own and resisted all my valiant efforts to control them. The tips crossed, the heels crossed, I stopped dead and then careered off at an alarming speed – and sideslipping is supposed to give you the maximum amount of control!

Your weight should be predominantly on the lower ski, although there must be enough on the upper one to stop it from waving around. When I was sideslipping with the right ski downhill, Jurgen told me to look down to the heel of my right boot, and to the left boot when that ski was nearest the valley. Apart from making me more aware of what should be happening with regard to weight distribution, it also forced me to lean away from the mountain with the appropriate shoulder. However, although this would work for a while, I'd soon lapse into my bad old ways and end up on my back again.

We went back to simple swing turns, starting with a snow plough and finishing with a small sideslip. I was still a lot better at turning to the right than to the left, but Jurgen just smiled in his understanding way and said, 'That's quite normal, Anneka. Everybody

dump skiers into the powder they love.

• *'Wild' snow* The type of snow sought by really diehard powder enthusiasts. It can consist of up to 90 per cent air and only 10 per cent snow, and in such conditions, it might be necessary to wear a face mask to avoid being suffocated by the spume thrown up by the skis. In reality, however, 'wild' snow is quite a rarity.

The courtesy code of the Fédération Internationale de Ski (FIS) states that a skier approaching another while traversing in the opposite direction should keep to the left of the oncoming skier.

Day 5 continued

has a sunny side.' Those words seemed to sum up our different attitudes towards my performance: to me, I was useless when turning to the left; to Jurgen, it was just not my 'sunny side'.

He told me to watch other people. It was true: the vast majority do have a 'sunny side'. In one direction, they moved smoothly and gracefully, but going the other way, they seemed to have hips made out of concrete. It was a relief to know that I wasn't alone.

Jurgen must have gone over the same ground with me a hundred times, and his patience would have impressed Job. 'Lean forward, weight over the downhill ski . . .' again and again. When I fell, he'd come and pick me up, ask if I was all right and somehow encourage me to go on. The only positive aspect of falling over was that I was able to watch my safety bindings in action. To my delight, they released without the slightest

discernible pressure on my ankles, and in my countless falls, I didn't seriously hurt myself once.

That day we skied down some of the steepest slopes I had encountered so far, so that, when I fell, I would often tumble for 20 yards or more. It was a curious feeling. I had seen skiers fall dramatically on television and I must have looked something like that, but there was no pain and no fear even though, theoretically at least, the mountainside was steep enough for me not to stop until I'd fallen all the way to St Anton.

My natural reaction was not to panic but to dig in with my heels in an effort to stop. There were times

Ingemar Stenmark

Almost every sport seems to have its superstars, and one of skiing's most notable is the Swede, Ingemar Stenmark, who has the sport in his blood – his father Eric was an Olympic racer and also competed at the 1956 and 1958 World Championships. Ingemar comes from Tarnaby, the same small village

that's the home of that other Swedish ace, Stig Strand. When these two raced as juniors, Strand usually came out on top, but when the dynamic duo joined the World Cup circuit, Stenmark took revenge for those early defeats and was virtually unbeatable at the slalom. Among many other things, he became known for mounting de-

Day 5 continued

when I found myself falling head-first down the slope, and then I would try to turn myself round and put my feet in a position to act as a brake. Jurgen said that I should try to make myself into a ball, with my feet pointing down the hill. 'Otherwise,' he said, 'you just get faster and faster.' In a strangely masochistic way, I was glad to have fallen so dramatically. At least I now knew that it was possible to look like a disaster without necessarily being one.

Every time I did eventually come to a halt, Jurgen would ski up to

vastating second runs that were rapidly tagged 'Stenmark charges'.

Fame quickly followed, and Stenmark developed into an internationally known star. However, back in his native Sweden, he's nothing short of a living legend. For example, due to popular demand, SAS, the national airline, had to broadcast Stenmark's races during their flights, and once, when the champion fell during a race and was unconscious for ten minutes, news of the event wiped the coverage of the General Election off the front pages of some of the country's major newspapers. Stenmark regularly beat Bjorn Borg in national polls to find Sweden's most popular sportsman, and it became a popular pastime to steal stones from his garden to keep as souvenirs!

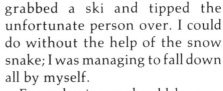

me carrying my skis, poles and whatever else I'd lost in the fall. I'd invariably look up at him and apologize for my stupidity, but he would equally invariably smile and silently help me back into my bindings. After one particularly unglamorous tumble, he asked me whether I had seen a snow snake. I looked alarmed – I had enough on my plate without having to worry about dangerous Alpine wildlife. However, with a sly smile, he went on to explain that the snow snake was a little creature that lived in the snow and only came out when a skier went past. It then

grabbed a ski and tipped the unfortunate person over. I could do without the help of the snow snake; I was managing to fall down all by myself.

Every beginner should be prepared for days like this. How nice it would be if modest but distinct progress were obvious every day, but this is rare. Jurgen wasn't nearly as discouraged as I was, and said that I was close to having two 'sunny sides'. He added that the slopes were steeper and we'd been skiing in more difficult snow than we'd seen up to now. I drew some comfort from that.

Lunch couldn't have come a moment too soon. Today we went to a hostelry just above the village – a converted farmhouse called the Krazy Kanguruh. The 'KK', as it is known, is famous throughout the skiing world, and if you went to St Anton without paying it a visit, it would be like going to Paris and giving the Eiffel Tower a miss.

The father of Alpine skiing

Mathias Zdarsky, born in Austria in 1856, is one of the major figures of ski mythology. Early in life, he lost an eye, but this did not hinder his drive to improve skiing technology. While working at an estate near Lilienfeld, he adapted the Norwegian running ski to Alpine terrain and developed a new type of binding.

However, Zdarsky became particularly renowned in the area of instruction, and his *Alpine (Lilienfelder) Ski Technique*, published in 1896, created a great deal of controversy, especially among the Scandinavians, because of his aim to introduce vast numbers of people quickly and safely to the sport. The Scandinavians, and particularly the Norwegians, had a much more

Day 5 continued

The KK is run by a crazy Swede called Gunnar Muenthe. Not only does he keep the madhouse of a bar in check, but he is also an accomplished skier, having been the coach of both the Canadian national team and the Swedish slalom team. All around the bar were photographs of famous skiers, including Franz Klammer and Ingemar Stenmark, as well as the four members of the Canadian team who are collectively known as the 'Crazy Canucks'. Craziness seems to be the order of the day at the KK.

Either by chance or to live up to its name, the bar was staffed by quite a few Australians, as well as by Brits, Canadians and even a few Austrians, and it could hardly be described as a quiet retreat. My few days at St Anton had shown me that long lunch breaks were the rule rather than the exception, and I was impressed by how extraordinarily friendly everyone seemed to be. Here at the KK, I was greeted enthusiastically by hordes of complete strangers – most of whom didn't have a clue who I was – and they made me feel very welcome indeed. This atmosphere was just what I needed to help get over the traumas of the morning.

I saw Carey and Liz at a table on the other side of the balcony, and I went over to join them for a *glühwein*. Liz said that she hadn't skied since the first day, and Carey admitted that she'd been grounded since Day 2 but, far from being unhappy about the situation, they were both having a lovely time. They just mooched around, taking things easy and spending longer in the bars. Liz would pack Brian off up the mountain in the morning and only meet up with him again at mealtimes. For her part, Carey had decided not to take up the option of private lessons after all, but said that she might get back on skis that afternoon and potter around on her own – but then

austere approach, and a fierce argument raged. To put an end to the squabbling, a giant slalom was held in 1905, which Zdarsky won by a large margin.

With the outbreak of World War I, the one-eyed Zdarsky, now nearing his 60th birthday, became an instructor in the Austrian army, but he was caught in an avalanche and suffered no fewer than 80 fractures and dislocations, including six separate injuries to his spine. Most people in a similar situation would not view the prospect of walking again with any degree of optimism, but Zdarsky was no ordinary person. Using special equipment that he designed himself, he trussed up his almost lifeless limbs and, to everyone's amazement, was able to ski again.

again, she might not. This proved that you can go on a skiing holiday and have a good time without actually doing any skiing.

It was good to meet other members of my class and find out how they'd been getting on. While I appreciated the value of private lessons in terms of making faster progress (in theory, at least), I missed the camaraderie of other people. Although, looking back, I

Some time after his death in 1940, a memorial to Mathias Zdarsky was set up in the mountains near Lilienfeld. On it is an epitaph written by the British 'ski knight', Arnold Lunn:

'Zdarsky will never be dethroned from his position as the father of Alpine skiing.'

Franz Klammer

Every sport produces a few magic moments, events that stand out from the countless hours of TV coverage we are subjected to each year. Most skiers would nominate Franz Klammer's final run in the Olympic downhill at Innsbruck as their sport's contribution to the

Day 5 continued

expect that I was at least keeping up with my former classmates, I had no way of knowing it then.

A shout from Gunnar summoned us outside. All heads were turned, and as I looked in the same direction, I saw him, ski clad, perched on the rail above the balcony and rocking gently back and forth. Then, with a blood-curdling cry, he leapt off the balcony like a kamikaze pilot and skied away down the slope.

Now I knew why it was called the Krazy Kanguruh.

It was quite extraordinary how, despite having had an awful morning, a couple of *glühweins* at lunch can make you raring to go again in the afternoon. Unfortunately, about half an hour later, on another run – this time down Happy Valley – I had returned to a state of deep depression.

Happy Valley it certainly wasn't – at least, not for me. The only thing that kept me going was the knowledge that there was only one way down. If I could have caught a bus or a taxi, my skis would have been off faster than it takes to down a Pear William. My ankles were aching and I was concentrating so hard that I got a headache. I felt like a bull in a china shop and lost count of the number of times I apologized to Jurgen.

On one occasion, when we hit a patch of deeper snow, I found myself stranded on a piece of high ground. Sideslipping was out of the question, I was not brave enough to point my skis down the mountain and ski my way out of trouble, and in the end, I tried to

Memory Hall of Fame. The flamboyant Austrian's performance enthralled skiers and non-skiers alike, and his bright yellow suit has become a vivid sporting image.

The year was 1976, and as Klammer waited to go on his last run, the brilliant Swiss, Bernhard Russi, was in the gold medal position with a seemingly unbeatable time of 1 minute 46.06 seconds. Klammer is reported to have asked his coach what he had to do to win. His answer: 'Throw yourself down the mountain and pray.'

What followed became skiing and TV history as the Austrian, with skis flying and arms flailing, propelled himself down the course with a mixture of courage, supreme skill

Day 5 continued

walk down in a reverse of a side-step. Jurgen then proceeded to tell me off for using my pole for support below my downhill ski, pointing out how easy it would have been to trap the pole under the ski – a very dangerous thing to do. Well, it seemed like a good idea at the time . . .

Jurgen tried absolutely everything to get me not to lean into the hill too much. He told me to stand firmly with my skis across the fall line, and then he stood just below

and the craziness of a man with a mission. His time at the finish was 1 minute 45.73 seconds - a time thought impossible by most sane people but one which secured the gold for Austria and confirmed Klammer as a folk hero in his native land.

While Klammer does have moments of sheer brilliance, he also has days of blatant ordinari-ness. However, when the selectors for the 1980 Olympics team announced, in one of the most controversial selection decisions in the history of the sport, that they preferred the more consistent expertise of Leonhard Stock rather than risk Klammer having one of his off weeks, admirers of the 1976 Olympic star were in an uproar. In fact, Olympic coach, Charlie Kahr,

Day 5 continued

me and took hold of my poles. 'I'm going to try and pull you over,' he said, 'and you have to stop me.'

I looked down into the valley and gulped, but although he pulled hard, I was able to resist.

'Now,' said Jurgen, 'look at your position.'

To my surprise, my knees were pressed firmly into the mountain, edging my skis severely, and my upper body and arms were leaning a long way into the valley.

'If you can lean over that far with me pulling you, and you still don't fall,' he said, 'then you should feel pretty safe about leaning out when you're skiing.'

Nice trick, Yogi, I thought, *but it's not that I don't know what to do, it's carrying it out that's the problem.* In my head, I'd already skied the perfect descent. There was no mystery to the theory, but the practice, I'd found, was a different story.

Finally Jurgen gave in and called it a day. I was exhausted. Despite the long lunch break at the Krazy Kanguruh, it had been a full day's skiing, and I shuddered to think how I would feel in the morning. I can't accurately describe what it felt like finally to ease out of my ski boots and slip into a pair of moon boots.

Back at the hotel, the sauna was sheer bliss, and I went down to dinner glowing with health and vitality. Physically, I felt great. The flabby bits I'd arrived with had hardened up, and I even discovered muscles in places where I didn't even know I had places.

There were to be no *après ski* frolics tonight. I went to bed early, happy and relaxed despite having had my worst day on the snow so far. In a way, I was just thrilled to be back in one piece. The misery and desperation that had seemed so real at the time had been left under a large snow drift somewhere up among the snow snakes. Tomorrow was another day.

had to have a police guard around his house, in addition to 'minders' for himself and his family, as protection against angry fans.

Despite this rejection by the powers-that-be, Klammer wasn't done yet, and he proved it in 1983, in an historic World Cup race at the Canadian resort of Lake Louise, near Banff in Alberta. Before it began, no fewer than eight skiers were in with a shot at the downhill title, but Klammer roared up from 15th to win in one of the closest finishes the sport has ever seen. Having seen off his seven rivals, the Austrian, adopting a Churchillian stance, stated: 'Never has it been so close, among so many, or the title won by so few points . . .'

DAY 6

Shall I go down for breakfast, or shall I spend an extra half an hour in bed? What a decision to start the morning with. Well, I wasn't hungry anyway, and as I rolled over and glanced out of the window, I saw that yesterday's sunshine and blue skies had been replaced by gloomy clouds and falling snow. *Maybe I'll stay in bed all day . . .*

However, although I eventually stirred a bit later than usual, I found myself, after a hot bath, ready to brave the conditions and head off for another day's skiing. (Besides, the film crew was waiting and I couldn't have got out of it even if I'd wanted to!) The high street was as crowded as ever, despite the atrocious weather. It seems that there's no such thing as a fair-weather skier. Everyone's enthusiasm was unquenchable.

Mountain conditions can be very changeable, and holidaymakers have to be prepared to take every day as it comes. Occasionally there are 'white-outs', when the weather is so bad that the authorities close the slopes and skiing is cancelled for the day. When this happens, many resorts offer alternative pastimes such as ice-skating, curling and tobogganing.

On the way to the ski school, I bumped into Peter, looking none the worse for wear despite the fact that he'd lost three of his pupils – Liz, Carey and me – within the first two days of the class, as well as having to cope with Andy's dramatic but ultimately unsuccessful attempts at learning to ski. When he discovered that I had no plans for the evening, he suggested that we get together after dinner,

Walk right up

No run is downhill all the way, and there will often be occasions when you need to do a bit of uphill climbing. Many skiers try to approach these inclines with enough speed to carry them over, but others, like me, often find themselves caught halfway up one side and having to stop themselves slipping backwards before climbing over the top.

One method of mounting a slope is to use the sidestep, the laborious technique that nearly finished me off on my first day of class. However, sidestepping has a number of other drawbacks in addition to the fact that it is extremely hard work and progress is very slow. You also have to manoeuvre yourself into a

position at right angles to the fall line, and this may be difficult for you as well as a danger to others. As you grind to a halt, you will usually find hordes of skiers flying towards you at all speeds and from all directions, most of them trying to ski the slope without stopping. The last thing they need is a beginner gingerly positioning him or herself directly across their path.

Jurgen showed me a good way to avoid becoming such a hazard, a method of walking straight up the fall line called the 'herringbone'. Open the tips of your skis into a kind of reverse snow plough and, keeping the inside edges biting into the snow, walk straight up the slope with a series of small steps.

It is important to make sure that you don't step on the heels of your

Day 6 continued

offering to show me a good time but refusing to tell me exactly what he had in mind. Throwing caution to the wind, I agreed.

Fortunately, I didn't keep Jurgen waiting in the falling snow for very long, and I think he was quite surprised that I'd turned up at all. For us, it was business as usual.

One thing soon became apparent. I really needed to change my sun glasses for a pair of goggles. There is nothing more annoying than flakes of snow landing on the

skis - that will bring you to an embarrassing standstill. Your climbing ski must always be clear of the standing ski before you bring the former down. Plant your sticks behind you for extra stability and try to keep moving. If you stop, you might begin to slip backwards. An expert at the herringbone can ski straight up to a slope and, in a single movement, walk up the hill, assisted by the forward momentum. It's bit ungainly, but it's a good way of making a quick ascent.

If you look back at the imprints you have made in the snow, it is easy to see how the herringbone got its name. The criss-cross pattern looks just like the tweed.

Day 6 continued

inside of the lenses and melting slowly down your cheeks. A pair of well-fitting goggles is a must – particularly in the colder months.

As we set off, one of the vehicles I'd often seen preparing the piste passed us on its way up the mountain. Jurgen said that it was called 'Ratrac', after the name of its manufacturer. He called over to the driver, and we hitched a lift up the slope. Now I'd experienced just about every form of mountain transport! (I should mention, however, that when I later told Professor Hoppichler about this convenient lift, he became quite angry, saying that you must *never* attach yourself to any of the vehicles that cross the snow. If you fell beneath the caterpillar tracks, it could be fatal.)

It was now my fifth day of tuition, and I found that I was being taught fewer new techniques, instead using the time for practice – mainly the basic swing turn, but also garlands and other simple manoeuvres – and consolidation. After the trials and tribulations of the day before, I was thrilled to discover that I was skiing with a great deal more style and confidence. Whether it was because of the extra sleep I'd grabbed, or because yesterday's instructions were only now sinking in, I don't know.

Whatever it was, I was really enjoying myself, and the sensation of cold snow falling on my face made the experience that much more exhilarating. I felt as if I'd made a real breakthrough. At last, I was in control and not wandering around like a lost sheep. I still managed to fall over several times, but it didn't seem to matter today, and I was quick to pick myself up and go for it again.

I had finally caught the bug. I was hooked.

Jurgen made me shorten my turns, and the narrower I made

In ski jumping, the technique of holding the arms in front of the body is called the 'bird style', whereas to hold them at the sides is known as the 'fish style'. In recent years, the latter has become almost universally employed.

my snow plough, the more I had to use my weight to turn. As a result, I began to swing from side to side in a hypnotic, flowing motion. The shorter turns created a kind of balletic rhythm, which was finally becoming instinctive. Jurgen then told me to reduce the weight on the back of my skis, and as I did, my posture automatically improved. I also found it easier to manoeuvre the skis, which was his original intention.

Almost without knowing it, I was making simple parallel turns. My skis were certainly staying together, so, yes, I must have been doing parallels. This is an important milestone for every skier. Not only is it a more efficient and satisfying class of turn, but it also takes the skier beyond the status of 'beginner' and into the more vague but impressive category of the 'intermediate'.

It's like learning to swim properly after only being able to dog-

Contrary to popular belief, it isn't the St Bernard that is used for mountain rescues. Instead, this is usually done by Alsatians (German Shepherds). They have a remarkable record: Swiss statistics show that, on the 305 occasions between 1945 and 1972 when dogs were used on mountain searches, the animals failed to find the victim, either dead or alive, only 36 times.

paddle, or, in the case of driving, like throwing away your L-plates. You can still be a terrible parallel skier, but it's not quite as obvious as seeing someone struggling to hold a wide and ugly snow plough. The latter makes the beginner stand out like a sore thumb, and the sooner it can be dispensed with, the sooner you'll find yourself with a happy skier on your hands. Some schools – for example, those that follow the French *ski évolutif* method – don't even include the snow plough in their training, choosing instead to teach the parallel turn from Day 1, using a succession of shorter skis.

We practised all morning, riding the T-bars and pottering around on the mountainside. Jurgen would try and get me to follow in his tracks, but by now I was keen to choose my own routes. I wanted to go where the mood took me, and on several occasions, it was Jurgen who ended up following me!

People say that learning to ski is like learning to ride a bicycle: once you've got over the initial problems of balance, staying upright and controlling your direction, it's dead easy. I couldn't pretend to be that proficient yet, but there was certainly a bright light shining for me at the end of the tunnel.

The morning passed quickly, although, without yesterday's blazing sun to warm us, I soon became quite cold. It was, therefore, a welcome relief when Jurgen led me to yet another *hütte* and I smelled the distinctive aroma of steaming hot *glühwein*.

Outside every *hütte* and bar, there is usually a forest of expensive equipment left unattended for hours, while the owners sit inside, knocking back the schnapps and *gulaschzuppe*. Ski resort tourist offices beg skiers always to take their poles with them into a bar, and to split up their skis, parking them paired off with those of a

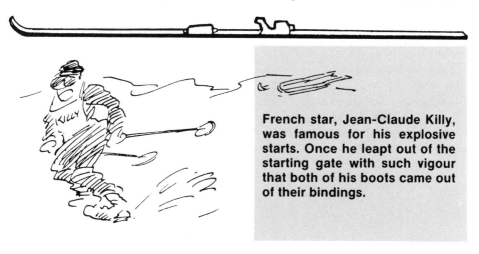

French star, Jean-Claude Killy, was famous for his explosive starts. Once he leapt out of the starting gate with such vigour that both of his boots came out of their bindings.

Day 6 continued

fellow-skier. Having lived in London for so long, where only fools would leave their cars unlocked for even a minute and still expect to come back and find the radio, I was sad to learn that ski thieving is getting worse each year. Here, the real trick after a good lunch is remembering where you left your skis!

As I sat with Jurgen in the bar, watching the thick snow falling outside, I was literally glowing with satisfaction. My instructor had always had faith in me, despite the débâcle of the previous day, and he was now sharing my excitement at seeing real progress. After this afternoon, there was still one day to go. *Where can I go from here?* I thought. *I only hope it isn't backwards again.*

Jurgen smiled and continued to said. 'You've come a long way for only your fifth day. Just think how you were on Sunday. You're now an expert!'

Jurgen should have got a gold medal for motivation, patience and sheer flattery – although calling me an 'expert' was a bit extravagant, even for him. He was right, though – I *had* made strides since those first tentative steps with Peter. That's one of the extraordinary things about learning to ski: it must be one of the few sports where a great deal of progress can be made in quite a short space of time.

Thinking about Jurgen made me realize how difficult being a ski instructor must be, particularly teaching beginners. With few exceptions, everyone must go through the same experiences: the excitement of discovering a new sport on the first day, the subsequent boredom of the nursery-slope routines, the thrill of the first real breakthrough, the disappointment of seeming to take a step backwards (usually just when you think you've cracked it) and then a day like today, when every-

The kamikazes

In France, they call it *ski extrême* ; in most other places, it is more commonly known as madness. It takes a special kind of skier to seek out the steepest slopes, the iciest rock faces and the most dangerous couloirs, and on a 'good' day, ice falls might have to be roped or crevasses jumped. Such is the ski extremist, surging ever upward beyond the point where even experienced mountaineers have turned back. This breed of skier makes the downhillers and hotdoggers look like OAPs queuing up for their pensions. They are the kamikazes of the mountains.

If you think that you would have to be, say, a bomb defuser or a lion tamer in your day job to be made of

thing seems to come together. The skiers all think their experiences are unique, but the truth is that the instructors go through it all again and again, week in, week out.

Time was passing and, reluctantly, we agreed to leave. I clicked back into my bindings and, with a thumbs-up to Jurgen, pulled down my goggles. We skied a short distance to a chair lift and then swung majestically up the mountain.

As we skied down, we came across a slalom course that had been set up on quite a steep slope. I was feeling a bit tired, and Jurgen and I decided to stop for a rest and watch a few of the runs. I could see a handful of ski instructors at the top – instantly recognizable in their distinctive red suits – and also several ordinary skiers, who probably made up an intermediate or even an advanced class. I'd thought that I'd been going quite fast until I watched these slalom skiers race down the mountain. Suddenly I realized that I was a

the stuff it takes to join this exclusive club, think again. Karl Pausch is a notorious daredevil, yet away from the frightening ice faces, he can be found going about his daily business as a bank clerk . . .

Perhaps the best-known extremists are Sylvain Saudan, a Swiss ski instructor, and Heini Holzer who comes from the Italian Tyrol. When he's not risking his neck on the slopes, the intrepid Holzer is a chimney sweep.

Saudan likes to be taken by helicopter to his starting point, whereas Holzer, never one to make life easy, prefers to climb there, saying it gives him a chance to study the conditions and to get himself 'fit for the descent'. 'Descent' is an understatement: these kamikazes seek slopes of between 50

Day 6 continued

tortoise compared to these hares.

This combination of skiers reminded me that you don't have to stop taking classes just because you've finally mastered the sideslip. However good you are, you can still go to a ski school and join a class with other skiers at a similar level. Your instructor will probably act more as a guide than as a teacher, taking you safely over some of the more difficult and exciting terrain, but even advanced skiers can brush up on their technique – there's always plenty to learn.

At the top of the course, a

and 60 degrees. To put that into perspective, the average recreational ski slope is between 20 and 30 degrees, and falls on the inclines frequented by the kamikazes are often fatal.

The steepest and iciest of the 'possible' Alpine faces is the Aiguille de Bionnassay, which rises to 13,300 feet in the Mont Blanc range on the French/Italian border. In October

1969, Saudan skied down it, overcoming an average incline of 55 degrees. Six months later, he took on the north ridge of the Eiger, arriving safely at the bottom one-and-a-half hours and 2,500 turns later.

Another risk-taker who likes to climb his mountain before embarking on the perilous downward journey is Patrick Vallençant. The Frenchman has also explained his

Day 6 continued

blond, red-suited skier was getting ready to go. At the signal, he took the first six or seven gates with great speed and accuracy, and even a novice like me could see that he was probably going to end up with the best time. However, as he crouched down to steer athletically round another gate, he suddenly lost his balance and was sent tumbling down the mountain. He came to a halt in a heap about 40 yards away from us, and lay there, motionless. Jurgen skied towards him, beckoning me to follow.

When we reached him, we could see that he was in great pain, and also was very angry with himself. He kept saying, *'Scheisse, scheisse,'* which needed no translation.

'It's Dieter,' Jurgen said to me as he knelt by the injured man's side, then turning his attention to his fellow instructor, he asked him where the damage was.

'I felt the tendons at the back of my knee snap as I went round that last pole,' Dieter replied through gritted teeth.

One of the other instructors who had now arrived on the scene radioed for a 'blood wagon' – the common name for the snow stretcher. Within 15 minutes, it had arrived, brought up by a combination of cable car and T-bar. Dieter was strapped in before being taken down to the village by two instructors from the school.

'He won't ski again this season,' predicted Jurgen ruefully, 'which means no money from teaching.'

It wasn't as bad as it sounded, for Jurgen admitted that there was a fund that helps to support ski instructors if they're put out of action through injury. However, when teaching is your livelihood, the greatest fear an instructor has is that of a serious fall – for both physical *and* financial reasons.

'Still,' Jurgen added, 'he might be able to do some teaching this summer.'

motives for extremism: 'When you ski a steep face or a tough couloir, you feel as big as the challenge.'

On slopes where one false move could result in death, concentration is the order of the day. Australian extremist John Falkiner has described what happens to him: 'In skiing the extreme, I find myself so focused that it is almost like meditation in motion. All outside thoughts leave, as my mind and body blend and function as one.'

Not surprisingly, Mount Everest represents the ultimate challenge to many kamikazes. For example, on a French expedition in 1978, Jean Afanassieff and Nicolas Jaeger skied from 26,900 to 20,340 feet. However, perhaps the most daring

Day 6 continued

'How can he? There won't be any snow.'

Jurgen explained that a lot of ski instructors go abroad when the Alpine season ends, taking their expertise to other parts of the world where the sport is still developing and which, because they lie below the Equator, have their winter during our summer. South America is a popular choice, and many graduates of the Austrian school can be found in the mountains of Chile, Bolivia and Argentina from May to September.

As we watched the blood wagon with Dieter on board making its way down towards the village, I shuddered as I remembered my father being similarly transported, and I decided to ski a little more carefully from then on.

I was beginning to get cold again, and could feel my performance suffering from my flagging concentration. Tiredness has a marked effect on your skiing, and it's always a good idea to do your more testing runs in the morning.

Jurgen, too, was not as enthusiastic as he had been before – perhaps Dieter's accident had affected him more than he had let on? We agreed to call it a day, and raced each other to the ski school where I screeched to a dramatic parallel stop. A perfect end to a near-perfect day.

After a delicious sauna, a short rest and an equally delicious dinner, I wrapped up well and waited for Peter to come and collect me, ready for just about anything he might have planned. However, when he arrived, he still refused to tell me what lay in store.

We got into his Jeep and headed out of the village, hurtling through the narrow streets at breakneck speed, accompanied as always by the sound of clattering snow chains. Eventually we pulled up by a large garage.

He led me up a winding moun-

feat in the history of skiing was undertaken by the Japanese extremist Yuichiro Miura, who in May 1970 attempted to ski Everest's South Col, a face so steep that no mountaineer had ever attempted to climb it.

A speed skier and a veteran of Chile's 'Flying Kilometre', Miura decided to use a parachute to slow himself down at the end of the run.

However, he knew that he had to reach a speed of 108 mph for the chute to be effective in the rarified atmosphere, and even then, he would have to have the wind blowing in his favour.

From his starting point at 26,516 feet, Miura completed the first part of the descent, to the South Col, without incident. It was on the second stage that the parachute

Day 6 continued

tain track with steep walls of snow on either side. Underfoot, a thin layer of snow covered a treacherous base of ice, and at times I had great difficulty keeping my feet. *What is Peter up to?* I asked myself. We must have walked for about 45 minutes, climbing higher and higher above the valley.

Eventually we arrived at a *hütte* perched on the mountainside. *This is a long way to come just for a schnapps*, I thought. It'd better be good inside.

In the dark, wood-panelled room, crowds of glowing *après skiers* milled boisterously around the bar. It was certainly a raucous atmosphere. In the middle of the room, a huge open fire, its smoke disappearing up a central chimney, provided a warming focal point.

We sat in the *hütte* for a couple of hours, swapping stories with our fellow revellers, everybody laughing and in good spirits. As there had been no cars outside, I assumed that everyone had made the

same long hike up the icy track to get here. That's loyalty for you. However, I still had a strange feeling that there was more to this place than met the eye, but whenever I questioned Peter, he just winked at me and ordered two more schnapps.

would be needed, to bring him safely to a halt before he hit the huge crevasse just above the Western Cwm. He set off, praying for a favourable wind.

When the time came to pull the ripcord, he felt, not the sharp tug of a healthily filled canopy, but the gentle rippling of a parachute struggling in thin air. In one horrible moment, he realized that the chute was not going to slow him down enough before he reached the crevasse. Then, suddenly, Miura hit a patch of uneven ground and fell, losing his skis and tumbling down the mountainside. When he finally came to rest, he was a mere 656 feet above the yawning crevasse. The man who had taken on the most dangerous face of Everest had survived.

123

Day 6 continued

Finally, it was time to go, and as I tottered to my feet, I remarked that I wasn't looking forward to the hike down the dark, icy mountain path.

'No problem,' said Peter. 'You don't have to.'

It was only then that I discovered his master plan. He hurried out of the bar, and the next time I saw him, he was holding something above his head like some big-game hunter's trophy: his prize was a flimsy-looking wooden toboggan. Of course, it all made sense now. I should have realized that the slippery, snow-walled path we had walked up was, when used in reverse, a toboggan run, just like the famous Cresta Run. I was nervous at the prospect of hurtling down it, but felt confident that Peter wouldn't let me come to any harm.

All but a few of us were quite tiddly, but that didn't deter anyone from crowding round the start and pairing themselves off for the big race. Peter sat at the front of our toboggan, and I seated myself behind him, clinging on for dear life. I hadn't been on a toboggan for many years, but soon rediscovered what great fun it was.

Suddenly, there was a pile-up in front of us, and despite Peter's skilled attempts to steer around

Austrian and Italian soldiers serving on the Alpine front during World War I discovered that it was much more effective to aim their fire at the slopes above the enemy rather than at the enemy themselves. Wilhelm Paulke, a ski instructor, serving with the German army at the time, estimated that 60,000 soldiers died during the war as a result of avalanches.

After his first ten minutes on skis at St Moritz in 1964 during the filming of *Help*, John Lennon was heard to say: 'That's enough for today. Let's all go to the restaurant.'

Holmenkollen in Norway is the home of ski jumping. When the World Cup circus comes to town, crowds of up to 100,000 people turn out to watch the flyers . . . and the fallers.

In an unofficial race after the first World Championships at Mürren in 1931, Esmé McKinnon, the 15-year-old British girl who had already won the downhill and slalom, sped towards the finish line near Lauterbrunnen Station. Before she could cross it, she saw a funeral procession leave the station and come up the hill towards her, so she stopped, moved to one side and respectfully allowed it to pass. Afterwards, the race committee unanimously agreed to subtract the time she had spent waiting from her overall time – and found that she had won that race as well.

Day 6 continued

the mêlée, we crashed into the tangled mass of bodies and toboggans, and both of us went flying. We landed in a heap and just lay there laughing like a couple of giggly school children. Nothing was broken, and we managed to rescue our toboggan from where it had come to rest, embedded in one of the high snow walls.

We remounted and sped on. At the bottom, Peter steered us round the last corner, and in a flash, I realized that the only way to stop was for both of us to dig in our heels . . . and pray. A cold shower of snow and ice hit our faces as we finally screeched to a halt, right next to the chained wheels of a very familiar-looking Jeep.

We were still laughing when we got back to the hotel. Tired but buzzing with excitement, I thanked Peter for a truly memorable evening and then crawled up to my room.

Nearly half of all injuries involve young skiers under the age of 18. Beginners of every age, who account for about 10 per cent of the skiing population, are involved in approximately a quarter of all injuries reported.

During the infancy of winter ski holidays, the season traditionally began on Christmas Eve and ended in the slush of the first Tuesday after Easter.

DAY 7

One piece of equipment you should always take on a skiing holiday is an alarm clock. Without mine, I would have been late for every one of my lessons. I may have cursed it every morning, but that mind-numbing *brrringgg* saved Peter and Jurgen a lot of waiting around.

It was Friday, my last day on the snow. Today I was going to report to Professor Hoppichler and show him how I'd got on during the week.

After a hearty breakfast, I met Jurgen outside the ski school, and we took the cable car to the nursery slope above the village. Blue skies had yesterday's fall of new snow. Jurgen said that some of the runs higher up the mountain had been closed because of the danger of avalanches.

I had arranged to meet the Professor at the Federal Ski School at St Christoph. This was almost a full morning's skiing away, so we first did a few warming-up exercises to loosen my weary muscles. They had worked hard all week but had come through with flying colours, despite having been asked to perform well beyond the call of duty.

I then made a few runs on the nursery slope, just to get used to the feel of the snow. It is always advisable to ease gently into the day's skiing, rather than jump straight out of bed and on to the most demanding ice-face. It was also extremely reassuring to be able to compare myself with the beginners struggling there in the nursery. I *had* come a long way.

We skied to a chair-lift station, and I discovered another unexpected skiers' injury: bruised knees. After a week of crashing through

Avalanche!

The sheer destructive power of an avalanche is underestimated by virtually all those who've never witnessed one at first hand. However, to think that it would be a simple task to claw one's way out of a covering of soft, fluffy snow could not be further from the truth.

An avalanche strikes with a force more terrible than a tidal wave - on an open slope, it can exert a pressure of 5,000 lb per square foot, and a cubic yard of compacted snow weighs almost a ton - and it's capable of destroying everything in its path. For example, when a piece of summit ice cap broke off the Huascaran in Peru in January 1962, the resulting avalanche travelled a distance of nine miles, wiping out

Day 7 continued

the turnstiles at T-bar, chair-lift and cable-car stations, I now had a couple of rather large bruises on my legs, which I rubbed soothingly as we headed up and away, over the shimmering snow.

Our journey to St Christoph gave us a good chance to review everything I'd done so far: swing turns, garlands, sideslipping, traverses, schussing and all the little exercises such as stepping up

six villages and partly destroying three others; the final death toll was over 4,000. Even some of the most unlikely places have felt the force of an avalanche: for instance, in 1836, one buried 15 people in their homes in Lewes, Sussex, killing eight of them.

But why do avalanches happen?

As well as coming in an infinite number of shapes and sizes, snow

flakes also take on certain characteristics depending on the temperature. In very cold conditions, they form into fine granules, while bigger and wetter flakes fall as the temperature rises. Once on the ground, the crystals undergo further changes according to prevailing atmospheric conditions.

Each successive snowfall may differ from previous ones and, as a

the slope and lifting alternate skis. Jurgen shouted instructions at every opportunity, cramming my head with as much coaching and advice as he could before I went back to England. He watched my every move like a hawk and was constantly talking to me.

Most of his comments were to do with my posture, which, sadly, was still in need of some improvement. Jurgen left no stone unturned: 'Your legs are too far apart ... You're leaning back too far ... You're *still* hugging the mountain!' By paying fanatical attention to detail, he was giving his pupil every possible chance of improving her skiing before she left St Anton.

Jurgen may have been a particularly conscientious instructor, but as a general policy, this kind of attention makes a lot of sense. Every ski resort earns its bread and butter from the holidaymakers who come back year after year. However, the learning process can

be very harrowing for some, and as I'd seen from Liz's and Carey's lack of enthusiasm, there is quite a high drop-out rate from beginners' classes. Some people never touch a pair of skis again if they have a bad experience on their first trip.

It is, therefore, in the interests of the resorts to make sure that beginners are well prepared and encouraged to go on to the next stage. The sooner they can go beyond that lowly status, the sooner they will really begin to enjoy the sport and want to indulge in it again and again. Although many people choose to take a skiing holiday at a different resort every year, a large number stay loyal to one centre, making it something of a second home. If a resort can sell itself on those terms, its cash registers will never stop ringing.

I wasn't skiing with the same inspired confidence that I'd had yesterday, and I began to wonder

consequence, may not bind firmly with each other. When these vast blankets of snow, often only delicately bound together, are no longer able to resist the pull of gravity, avalanches can and do occur. The situation is often aggravated by changing temperature and/or wind conditions, which make the layers even more unstable.

The dry, loose snow avalanche is

the least dangerous type, as it starts from a single point and usually involves only the top layer of snow. However, if the snow becomes airborne (as it can after a snowfall), this can present a much greater danger. The snow then quickly picks up speed – it can reach a velocity of up to 200 mph – and produces powerful shock waves.

Another type of avalanche is the

APRES SKI

wet snow variety. These usually occur in the spring, when a heavy mass of solid wet snow parts company with its mountain host and begins its relentless journey down.

However, it's the slab avalanches that are responsible for the majority of serious accidents. They happen when the wind has packed the snow into an unstable layer resembling a vast, hard slab. This can be attached to the mountain in the most delicate way, often at just a few critical points, and the slightest vibration can cause fractures that send great masses of compacted snow crashing down. There can be few more heart-stopping sounds than the terrifying *crack* that accompanies a slab fracture. This informs you that, soon, huge lumps of concrete-like snow will be hurtling into a valley.

Day 7 continued

whether I'd passed my peak. Tired legs and difficulty in concentrating contributed to a sloppier performance, and I thought that, maybe, one week is enough for a beginner like me. There's a lot to take in the first time round, and I imagined that, after a break and an opportunity to digest everything, I'd come back a better skier next time. I'd have to wait and see, but one thing was certain – I *would* be back.

We'd skied for nearly two hours when, from our vantage point high on the mountain, Jurgen pointed to a cluster of vividly coloured buildings in the valley below, which looked like a little lunar outpost.

'There – look,' he said. 'That's St Christoph.'

The route down was quite easy, and for the most part, I was able to relax and just enjoy myself. The final approach to the village was a wide area of well-prepared piste,

down which I made long sweeping turns. However, I still had a 'sunny side', and the tiring descent was peppered with occasional falls. By the time I skied up to the futuristic igloo that is St Christoph's focal point, my thighs were really aching.

Professor Hoppichler was there to meet us, and despite the state of my lower limbs, I was able to create a good impression as I came to a very professional-looking stop right in front of him. I was thrilled when he complimented me, but I told him that I owed everything to my instructor. 'He's a star,' I said.

'No, you're the star,' came the reply. I couldn't get over how nice everyone had been that week.

'Now I have a present for you,' said the Professor, pointing to the brow of a hill. 'Look up there.'

In the distance, I could see a group of skiers, all dressed in the smart scarlet uniforms of the National Bundesportheim. They

Alpine regions are at risk of slab avalanches, as are some areas of Scotland where high winds build up slab snow on sheltered lee slopes.

The average holiday skier will usually have no reason to feel in any particular danger. Experienced local experts continually monitor the conditions and, long before skiers have tasted their muesli in

the morning, they'll often blast away dangerous build-ups of snow to make sure that the pistes are safe.

Even space technology has lent a hand in avalanche control. Research carried out by the US National Aeronautics and Space Administration has aided the identification of mountain areas that are at risk from avalanches: in NASA satellite photo-

graphs, dangerous slopes show up in a different colour, indicating a different temperature.

Providing you pay strict attention to all the warning signs and under no circumstances attempt to ski on an area that's been closed off, you should come to no harm and never have to experience that frightening race down the mountain, with tons of snow at your heels. Trust the locals: they'll invariably know the mountains and the conditions much better than you. You may not be able to see why a tempting area of harmless-looking fresh snow has been designated a 'no go' area, but you can rest assured that whoever closed off the area had an excellent reason for doing so.

Day 7 continued

seemed to be waiting for something. Suddenly, I heard the crackle of a great Tannoy system being turned on, and then music – first, a classical piece, and then a bit of Euro rock – blared out over the mountains.

The skiers set off from the top of the hill and, in perfect formation, skied down the slope in a number of choreographed routines – two of them, then three, four and finally the whole group making intricate cross-over patterns in time to the music. Some of the skiers made wide swings, while others were doing quick athletic ones, which appeared to be made from the hips down. I asked Professor Hoppichler what this manoeuvre was.

'Oh, that's the *wedeln*,' he replied (*there's a description of this on pages 138 and 139*).

The entire display was very impressive – the skiing version of the Red Arrows.

After the show, we went into the igloo (which turned out to be a bar) for lunch and some much-needed liquid refreshment. The glass dome acted like a greenhouse, and I'm sure the sales of beer rocketed on hot sunny days. Jurgen and the Professor had snatched a few muted words outside, and now my instructor told me that there was still one thing I had to do. Professor Hoppichler nodded, smiling.

After our meal, we said our farewells to the Professor, and headed for the cable car that would take us to our mystery destination. As the car pulled us upwards and the psychedelic buildings disappeared far below us, it felt as if we were blasting off for the moon.

In a resort area as developed as this one, it would be very easy to get lost in the mountains, what with the multiplicity of routes and lifts, and without Jurgen, I

You should also learn how to recognize potentially dangerous conditions. Any slope of more than 15 degrees can be at risk if covered by one or more layers of unstable snow. This can occur anywhere: it's a mistake to think that only the most inaccessible parts of a mountain are prone to avalanches. Areas near lifts or even innocuous-looking pistes can be a danger, so it's vital to heed all notices and warnings.

If you're skiing off-piste and you come to a place that you or your guide feels might be a potential avalanche hazard, there are a number of steps you can take that will reduce the danger. First, stay as high as possible on ridges, or move to terrain that is broken by

wouldn't have had a clue where I was going. Until you become experienced at reading piste maps, you should always ski with someone who knows the region.

A word of warning: the only official ski guides are those attached to the ski school, and the authorities don't look kindly on unauthorized guides taking work

trees or rocks, which will serve to anchor the snow better. Avoid cornices as well as slopes that end in a steep drop. Also to be avoided are gullies, where even a small slide can bury a victim in deep snow.

If you can't avoid crossing dangerous ground, take your hands out of the straps of your poles (so that you can discard them if you

need to) and proceed, one at a time. Follow the most direct route away, which may involve going straight down rather than traversing.

It is safest to cross on foot rather than on skis. The latter can have an effect similar to that of a glass cutter's scoring knife, causing a shallow fracture which then puts more stress on the next layer. This

Day 7 continued

away from the school. In the past, many chalet girls have been re-primanded for making off with paying customers in this way. In addition, only an official guide would be fully aware of the condition of the slopes and, especially, of any dangers such as avalanche hazards.

At the end of our cable-car journey, we skied a short distance – to another cable-car station. I looked enquiringly at Jurgen, but he just smiled secretively. Then I looked up to where this cable car would take us . . . and up and up.

'*Oh, no,*' I moaned.

'Oh, yes!' replied Jurgen trium-phantly.

'Not the *Valluga!*' I wailed.

'Come now, Anneka, I'm sure you're ready. I wouldn't ask you to do it if you weren't.'

I knew that, if they wanted to gain any 'piste cred', skiers were expected to ski down the Valluga at the end of their first week's skiing. But, somehow, I'd never thought that this would apply to me. Frankly, I became dizzy just looking up the mountain – which simply towers over St Anton – and

too fractures and transfers the stress to the snow beneath it, and the process can continue until an entire section of snow finally breaks off.

If you're caught in a avalanche but think it may be possible to ski clear, do so with the minimum of delay. If you can't avoid it, discard your skis, poles and rucksack and look for the best place to shelter – ideally, in among trees or behind rocks. Getting rid of your equip-ment will greatly increase your chances of survival.

If you become engulfed in the snow, try to treat the avalanche as a tidal wave and 'swim' on the sur-face, keeping your mouth closed. As the avalanche comes to a halt, create a breathing space for your face and chest, and push anything you can – skis, poles, an arm or legs

136

watching the minuscule figures of skiers making their way down from the summit.

Oh well, I thought, *this is meant to be 'The Adventure Series'. Just don't let me break a leg on my last day!*

The journey up by cable car was glorious. It was incredible to look out over the tops of all the nearby mountains and to see the miles and miles of runs dotted with tiny skiers. When the car finally stopped it was like being on top of the world. I felt exhilarated and terrified!

The journey down starts off with a gentle blue run, although the first twenty yards or so were very steep and I took my first dive within seconds. It was my usual problem – people. Surely a girl deserves a bit of peace and quiet at a crisis time like this! The man in question seemed to be heading straight for me but, supremely confident, shot past me with a flick of his hips at the last moment.

'That was one of my better falls,' I quipped unsteadily as Jurgen helped me to my feet.

'That wasn't your fault,' he replied. But, never one to allow an opportunity to further his pupil's

– through to the surface. This will create an air passage and will also mark your position for rescuers.

Although the awesome power of an avalanche can easily break limbs and crush fragile bones, the most common cause of death is suffocation. In fact, anyone completely buried in snow has between 15 and 20 minutes to be found and excavated before all the air is gone.

Survivals are the exception rather than the rule.

If you're part of a search party looking for an avalanche victim, you'll first need to mark his or her last position. Search the area thoroughly, proceeding as quietly as you can and using reversed ski poles to probe the snow. Always be aware of the danger of further avalanches.

education to pass by, he added, 'When you came down that run, your legs were too far apart. They should have been almost together.'

Back upright again, we carried on down to a T-bar. All my thoughts had been so focused on getting down the mountain I couldn't believe I had to go up again! But up we went to the most difficult section of the journey – a rather ominous-looking red run, tapering off into the distance into a wide cruising piste. I longed for the day when I could ski the mountain effortlessly without stopping and starting as I was still having to do and I must have exasperated Jurgen by falling into old habits of long traverses and snow-plough turns. However, much of the journey was on slopes no worse than any others I'd skied during the week and I began to feel increasingly confident.

Eventually we came to a 'motorway' section, seemingly jam packed with skiers of all levels and, as usual, I tried to moderate my descent by doing swing turns. This was a mistake. The swings took me across the piste – and right into the path of a very annoyed green-suited skier, who almost flattened me. As he whooshed round me, an angry look on his face, I decided, *If you can't beat 'em, join 'em*, and, tucking my poles under my arms, and assisted by a little push from Jurgen, I sped down the mountain faster than I would have believed possible. It was amazingly exhilarating and I arrived at the bottom breathless and triumphant.

Jurgen said that I now deserved a reward, and this, you won't be amazed to hear, turned out to be a visit to yet another *hütte* . . . and a noisy one at that. Long before I could see where it was coming from, I could hear a cacophony of raucous shouts, mixed with the *oompah* of traditional Austrian music. I'd thought I'd experienced

Wagging
the serpent's tail

The technique of swinging the knees from side to side in a series of smooth, fluid movements is known in Austria as the *wedeln*. It was introduced to the world in the 1950s – I learned later that Professor Hoppichler was a member of the Austrian Ski Demo Team that first demonstrated it – and is one of the most beautiful techniques to watch and one of the most satisfying to do, although it does require strong legs and a good sense of rhythm and balance.

Day 7 continued

just about everything the hostelries of the region could offer, from the mania of the Krazy Kanguruh to the most quaint Tyrolean restaurant. What surprises did this place have in store?

Our host was a red-nosed character dressed in *lederhosen* and a leather apron. In one corner, there was a band comprising a motley selection of musicians, all similarly attired and sporting equally red noses. The accordion player, apparently the leader, led the sozzled throng in a bout of exuberant community singing.

They played a number of traditional songs, including one called *'Schnee, schnee'*, which I dedicated to the two streakers who had given me such a shock at the sauna door on Tuesday. Everybody seemed to know all the words except me, of course, but I picked up on some of the choruses and mouthed along confidently to the rest.

There were obvious favourites and established routines. At one point, everyone stood on their chairs and lifted their tables. Given the state everyone seemed to be in, it was a miracle that the 20 or so glasses of beer, schnapps and *glühwein* perched precariously on our table did not end up on the floor. There were a few crashes from the other side of the bar, followed by loud cheers, so I guess they weren't so lucky.

A middle-aged woman, who looked as if she might be a solicitor's PA back in sober England, then staggered up to the microphone and declared that she was

Wedeln literally means 'tail-wagging', and its short swings leave a snake-like pattern in the snow, which probably accounts for the name of a similar technique found in France - *le serpent*. It is enjoyed by millions, particularly slalom racers who have to negotiate narrowly spaced gates as quickly as possible.

The action of the upper body will vary according to conditions. On steeper slopes, you may need to unweight your skis with an upward movement, while on more gentle inclines, you should be able to glide easily and still keep the upper body

going to sing us all a song. (I thought I heard the sound of her husband disappearing under the table with embarrassment!) 'I'm going to sing "My Way",' she announced, and she certainly kept her word. In the space of two short verses, she overtook slab fractures as the single greatest potential cause of avalanches. There were, however, no critics in that crowd, and once she'd done it *her* way for the last time, she received a rapturous ovation.

'quiet'. For extra stability, the poles should be planted near the inside ski as you rapidly change edges.

It's fun to develop a regular rhythm and ski in time with a companion. However, the ultimate pleasure is *wedeln*ing in deep, virgin snow and looking back to see the wiggly tracks you've left on the previously untouched mountainside.

The most prestigious event in the ski-jumping calendar is known as the 'Four Hills'. This event comprises jumps at Oberstdorf, Bischofschofen and Garmisch–Partenkirchen in West Germany and Innsbruck in Austria.

Day 7 continued

Our host bobbed over and began collecting people for the inevitable conga. (I would like to state here and now that, had it not been for the filming, at this juncture I would have fled back to the slopes and the real world!)

Once we'd snaked our way round the bar, it was time to go outside. However, to use the door would have been far too conventional – so through a window we went. Outside, the cold air came as quite a shock. I then realized that I'd been unfortunate to be immediately behind our host. For his *pièce de résistance*, he reached between his legs and grabbed tight hold of my hand. I couldn't remove it, so as it was clearly the done thing, I reached through my legs with my free hand and fished around for the waiting one of the person behind me. I made sure that I held that hand tightly – I wanted to know exactly where it was at all times. All the way down the line, my fellow revellers were becoming attached in this intimate way. We must have looked a funny sight, and not surprisingly, we couldn't keep the position for very long. Back inside, we eventually collapsed in a heap in the middle of the floor.

It had become obvious to me that a skiing holiday can be anything to everybody. You can be dedicated skier and take that part seriously, or an equally dedicated fun worshipper, where the skiing is only important as a means of getting from one bar to another. Luckily, most people find some middle ground.

It was only a short run down to the school, but as I collected my skis Jurgen gave me a warning. This was, he said, going to be the infamous 'last run of the last day', when an alarmingly high percentage of accidents happen. People become over-confident and relax their concentration, and that's when you're at your most vulnerable. I'd made it this far – I'd even

Five-times British cross-country champion, John Moore, bit away all his front teeth while fighting his way to victory over the exhausting courses.

Although he was by then in his mid-40s, former French racing champion, Jean-Claude Killy, completed the 1982 New York marathon in under four hours.

skied down the Valluga! – and was determined not to do anything stupid. I just hoped that the schnapps didn't have other ideas.

Dusk was falling and I skied down mainly on instinct. I'm sure my style would have drawn howls of criticism from the purists, but I got to the bottom in one piece, which was the main thing.

It was time for Jurgen and me to make our farewells. The least he deserved for his efforts was a kiss, which he received somewhat self-consciously. He'd been perfectly charming for the last four days, and had seen me through both demoralization and euphoria. I knew that what I'd achieved was largely down to him. It was surprising how hard it was to say good-bye, but then, we *had* been through quite a lot together.

However, with a wave, we parted, and I carried my skis back to Tony's store for the last time. As the ski boots came off, I made sure that I savoured that heavenly moment for a final time.

I felt that the week had been rounded off nicely. Some people grab a last run on the Saturday morning, but I thought I'd call it a day while I was still on top. Ski passes are normally only valid until the Friday, so if you want to ski on Saturday, you have to buy a special half-day pass. There are also stories of people being stranded up the mountain and missing their coach to the airport. Worse still, skiing again would have meant another 'last run of the last day': some have serious accidents only minutes before they're due to go home. No, for me, Saturday morning would be spent having a lie-in, a long breakfast and a leisurely pack. As the snow began to fall again outside, I went up to my room and reflected on the week. I'd certainly overcome a number of my fears. For a start, the equipment had shown itself to be both safe and

Canadian downhiller, Laurie Graham, lost no time in her quest to become one of the world's top women competitors: she started skiing at the age of four, was racing by the time she was nine, at 14 was named to the Southern Ontario team, and at 17 was included in the national team for the Can–Am finals.

In the first Winter Olympics at Chamonix in 1924, Norway won 11 of the 12 medals for skiing. The only one that evaded the Norwegians was the bronze in the 18-kilometre cross-country event.

Day 7 continued

reliable. I also realized that I could fall without hurting myself – I'd proved it on innumerable occasions! – and, to a certain degree, I'd learned how to be in control of my skis and how to stop almost whenever and wherever I wanted to. There was, however, one outstanding fear: other people. I hadn't been aware of just how crowded a mountainside can be, and how you have to be alert at all times to avoid causing, or becoming part of, a major catastrophe.

If you catch your ski tip while skiing at 30 mph, you have precisely 34.6 milliseconds for your bindings to release before your knee ligaments rupture!

A slalom gate placed down the fall line is said to be 'closed', whereas a gate set across the fall line is regarded as 'open'.

A snow-making machine turned a mound of bomb rubble in Berlin into a totally artificial mountain.

Day 7 continued

The biggest advance I'd made, however, was the fact that I was now hooked, something I never thought I'd be. I doubt if I'll ever be a great skier, but I know that I'll enjoy my next skiing holiday, feeling confident that I could now more than hold my own in a party of friends.

So I'd learned to ski and got a healthy tan into the bargain. The physical exertion and the mountain air also leave you glowing with vitality, and it was encouraging to see such a wide range of people, old and young, taking part in such a healthy pursuit. Even the Brits, who sometimes seem to be the laziest people in the world, appeared to find a new lease of life.

Yes, the world of skiing has a new convert. Tomorrow, as I fly out over the mountains, back to London, I'll take with me a sackful of memories to look back on and enjoy until the day when I snap back into my bindings and pull down my goggles at the top of the next blue run . . .